Miss Jess VR Curriculum Empathy and Inclusion

Miss Jess

Published by Think N Grow Big Publishing, 2024.

MISS JESS VR CURRICULUM EMPATHY AND INCLUSION

First edition. September 11, 2024.

Copyright © 2024 Miss Jess.

ISBN: 979-8227097408

Written by Miss Jess.

To my beloved daughters, whose curiosity and resilience inspire me every day. You are the reason I strive to create a world filled with empathy and understanding.

To my mother, whose unwavering support and wisdom have guided me through every challenge. Your strength and love are the foundation upon which I build my dreams.

To my grandmother, whose legacy of kindness and perseverance continues to light my path. Your stories and values remind me of the power of generations working together for change.

May this curriculum be a testament to the power of family, the importance of embracing our differences, and the incredible impact we can make when we unite across generations to create a better, more inclusive world.

Jess Toft Founder Think N Grow Big & Miss Jess VR

Vision and Mission

Vision: To create a world where every individual, regardless of their background or abilities, has access to inclusive and equitable education.

Mission: To empower educators, parents, and communities to foster environments that support neurodivergent individuals and promote empathy, understanding, and inclusivity.

Miss Jess VR Curriculum Index

1. Introduction
   - Overview of the Curriculum
   - Objectives and Goals
   - Importance of Empathy in Education
   2. Module 1: Understanding Empathy (Weeks 1-6)
   - Week 1: Introduction to Empathy
   - Week 2: Key Concepts and Definitions
   - Week 3: Activities and Exercises
   - Week 4: VR Experiences and Simulations
   - Week 5: Reflection Questions
   - Week 6: Empathy in Daily Life
   3. Module 2: Cultural Sensitivity (Weeks 7-12)
   - Week 7: Importance of Cultural Sensitivity
   - Week 8: Understanding Different Cultures
   - Week 9: Interactive VR Scenarios
   - Week 10: Reflection and Discussion
   - Week 11: Case Studies
   - Week 12: Celebrating Cultural Diversity
   4. Module 3: Community Service (Weeks 13-18)

Empathy and Inclusion Curriculum

Introduction

Empathy is the ability to understand and share the feelings of others. It is a crucial skill for building strong, compassionate communities and fostering positive relationships. This curriculum is designed to help students develop empathy through diverse perspectives, interactive activities, and real-world applications. By engaging in this program, students will learn to recognize and appreciate the emotions and experiences of others, leading to a more inclusive and understanding environment.

Objective

To foster empathy, understanding, and compassion among students through diverse perspectives, interactive activities, and real-world applications.

Grade Level

Applicable for K-12, with modifications for age-appropriate content and activities.

Duration

Year-long program with 40 weekly sessions.

Key Objectives

1. Promote Awareness and Understanding:

○ Conduct workshops and seminars to educate about neurodivergence and Autism Spectrum Disorder (ASD).

○ Develop and distribute educational materials that highlight the importance of inclusivity.

2. Support Educators and Parents:

○ Provide resources and training for educators to implement inclusive teaching strategies.

○ Offer support groups and counseling for parents of neurodivergent children.

3. Advocate for Policy Changes:

○ Collaborate with policymakers to create and enforce laws that support inclusive education.

○ Participate in global forums and summits to advocate for the rights of neurodivergent individuals.

Programs and Initiatives

1. Inclusive Education Workshops:

● Description: Interactive workshops designed to equip educators with the skills and knowledge to create inclusive classrooms.

● Target Audience: Teachers, school administrators, and educational support staff.

● Activity: Participants will engage in role-playing scenarios to practice inclusive teaching strategies.

● Self-Reflection: Participants will reflect on their current teaching practices, identify areas for improvement, and set personal goals for fostering inclusivity.

2. Parent Support Groups:

● Description: Regular meetings for parents to share experiences, gain insights, and receive emotional support.

● Target Audience: Parents and guardians of neurodivergent children.

● Activity: Group discussions and sharing sessions facilitated by a trained counselor.

● Self-Reflection: Parents will reflect on their parenting strategies, consider how they can better support their neurodivergent children, and set personal goals for improvement.

3. Advocacy and Policy Engagement:

● Description: Initiatives aimed at influencing educational policies to ensure they are inclusive and equitable.

● Target Audience: Policymakers, educational leaders, and advocacy groups.

● Activity: Workshops and seminars on effective advocacy techniques and policy analysis.

● Self-Reflection: Participants will reflect on their role in advocating for policy changes, assess their current advocacy efforts, and set goals for more effective contributions.

Conclusion

By fostering empathy, understanding, and inclusivity, we can create a world where every individual has the opportunity to thrive. Join us in our mission to make a positive impact on the lives of neurodivergent individuals and their families.

Introduction Letter for Miss Jess's VR Empathy and Inclusion Curriculum

Dear Students,

Welcome to a journey that I hope will transform the way you see the world and interact with those around you. This curriculum is more than just a series of lessons; it is a reflection of my own experiences and the values I hold dear. I am thrilled to share this with you and to embark on this adventure together.

My passion for empathy and inclusion began at a young age. Growing up, I often felt like an outsider, struggling to find my place in a world that seemed to move too fast and too harshly. It was through the kindness of a few empathetic individuals that I found my voice and my confidence. These experiences taught me the profound impact that empathy can have on someone's life.

My journey in education has been diverse and deeply fulfilling. I started in early childhood education, where I learned the importance of nurturing empathy from a young age. As a Teacher, Center Director and Substitute Teacher Manager, I saw the challenges and triumphs of educators and students alike, and I realized the critical role empathy plays in creating supportive learning environments. Working as a Special Education Educational Assistant, I witnessed the incredible resilience and potential of students with diverse needs, further solidifying my commitment to fostering inclusion.

One of the most profound influences on my approach to empathy and inclusion has been my experience as a mother of a child on the autism spectrum. This personal journey has taught me the importance of understanding and accommodating different sensory experiences and perspectives. It has driven me to create a curriculum that not only teaches empathy but also immerses students in diverse scenarios, allowing them to truly walk in someone else's shoes.

As I delved deeper into my studies and career, I realized the potential of innovative technologies like Virtual Reality (VR) and Artificial Intelligence (AI) to enhance learning experiences. I envisioned a curriculum that not only teaches empathy but also immerses students in diverse perspectives and scenarios, allowing them to truly walk in someone else's shoes. This vision led to the creation of the VR Empathy and Inclusion curriculum you are about to explore.

Throughout this curriculum, you will engage in activities that challenge you to think critically, feel deeply, and act compassionately. You will explore various fields, from politics and business to science and the arts, all through the lens of empathy. You will use VR to experience different perspectives and develop a deeper understanding of the world around you.

My hope is that this curriculum will inspire you to become empathetic leaders and advocates for inclusion in your communities. Remember, empathy is not just about understanding others; it's about taking action to make a positive difference. Each of you has the power to create a more compassionate and inclusive world.

Thank you for joining me on this journey. I am excited to see the incredible impact you will make as you embrace empathy and inclusion in your lives.

With heartfelt gratitude and anticipation, Miss Jess

Miss Jess VR Curriculum
Empathy and Inclusion

Week 1 Lesson Plans Day 1: Understanding Emotions

Objective: Students will learn to identify and name different emotions, understand

their impact, and develop emotional literacy.

Activities:

1. Emotion Identification:

○ **Traditional:** Use emotion cards with different facial expressions. Students pick a card and describe a time they felt that emotion.

○ **VR:** Create a VR scenario where students interact with characters displaying various emotions. Students identify and discuss the emotions.

○ **Reflection Activity:** After the activity, students write a short reflection on how recognizing and naming their emotions can help them in their daily lives.

2. Emotion Journaling:

○ **Traditional:** Students keep a journal to record their emotions daily and reflect on what triggered them.

○ **VR:** Use a VR journaling app where students can visually represent their emotions and triggers.

○ **Reflection Activity:** At the end of the week, students review their journal entries and write a reflection on any patterns they noticed and how they can manage their emotions better.

3. Group Discussion:

○ **Traditional:** Hold a class discussion on how different emotions affect behavior and relationships.

○ **VR:** Host a virtual group discussion in a VR classroom setting, allowing students to share their experiences in a safe space.

○ **Reflection Activity:** Students write a reflection on what they learned from the discussion and how they can apply it to their interactions with others.

Day 2: Perspective-Taking

Objective: Students will practice seeing situations from others' perspectives to foster empathy.

Activities:

1. Role-Playing:

○ **Traditional:** Students role-play different scenarios where they must see things from another person's perspective.

○ **VR:** Use VR simulations where students can step into the shoes of different characters and experience their viewpoints.

○ **Reflection Activity:** After the role-playing, students write a reflection on how it felt to see things from another person's perspective and how it might change their behavior.

2. Storytelling:

○ **Traditional:** Read stories that highlight diverse perspectives and discuss the characters' experiences.

○ **VR:** Create or use existing VR stories that immerse students in different cultural and social contexts.

○ **Reflection Activity:** Students write a reflection on how the stories changed their understanding of different perspectives and what they learned about empathy.

3. Perspective-Taking Exercises:

○ **Traditional:** Use worksheets with scenarios requiring students to describe how others might feel.

○ **VR:** Develop interactive VR exercises where students make choices based on understanding others' perspectives.

○ **Reflection Activity:** Students write a reflection on how practicing perspective-taking can improve their relationships and interactions with others.

Day 3: Active Listening

Objective: Students will learn and practice active listening skills to enhance empathy.

Activities:

1. Listening Techniques:

○ **Traditional:** Teach techniques like paraphrasing, summarizing, and asking open-ended questions.

○ **VR:** Use VR modules that simulate conversations, allowing students to practice and receive feedback on their listening skills.

○ **Reflection Activity:** Students write a reflection on which listening techniques they found most effective and how they plan to use them in real-life conversations.

2. Listening Pairs:

○ **Traditional:** Pair students to share stories while their partner practices active listening.

○ **VR:** Create VR environments where students can pair up and practice listening in different scenarios.

○ **Reflection Activity:** After the activity, students write a reflection on how it felt to be truly listened to and how they can improve their listening skills.

3. Impact of Listening:

○ **Traditional:** Discuss how active listening can improve relationships and resolve conflicts.

○ **VR:** Use VR scenarios to demonstrate the positive impact of active listening in various contexts.

○ **Reflection Activity:** Students write a reflection on how active listening can change their interactions and relationships for the better.

Day 4: Inclusivity and Diversity

Objective: Students will understand and celebrate differences, promoting inclusivity.

Activities:

1. Diversity Awareness:

o **Traditional:** Use activities like cultural presentations and discussions on diversity.

o **VR:** Create VR experiences that immerse students in different cultures and lifestyles.

o **Reflection Activity:** Students write a reflection on what they learned about diversity and how they can promote inclusivity in their community.

2. Inclusivity Projects:

o **Traditional:** Develop projects where students work together to create inclusive environments.

o **VR:** Use VR platforms to collaborate on virtual projects that promote inclusivity.

o **Reflection Activity:** After completing the projects, students write a reflection on the importance of inclusivity and how they can continue to support it.

3. Empathy towards Neurodivergent Individuals:

o **Traditional:** Educate students about neurodiversity and how to support neurodivergent peers.

o **VR:** Create VR simulations that help students understand the experiences of neurodivergent individuals.

○ **Reflection Activity:** Students write a reflection on what they learned about neurodiversity and how they can be more supportive and inclusive.

Day 5: Empathy and Inclusion in Action

Objective: Students will apply empathy and inclusion in real-life and virtual scenarios.

Activities:

1. Community Service:

○ **Traditional:** Participate in community service projects that require empathy and teamwork.

○ **VR:** Use VR to simulate project planning activities, allowing students to practice empathy in virtual settings.

○ **Reflection Activity:** After the community service activities, students write a reflection on how the experience helped them understand the importance of empathy and inclusion.

2. Conflict Resolution:

○ **Traditional:** Teach conflict resolution techniques and role-play scenarios.

○ **VR:** Develop VR scenarios where students must resolve conflicts using empathy and inclusion.

○ **Reflection Activity:** Students write a reflection on how they can use empathy and inclusion to resolve conflicts in their own lives.

3. Empathy in Leadership:

○ **Traditional:** Discuss the role of empathy in leadership and provide examples.

○ **VR:** Use VR scenarios to demonstrate empathetic leadership in action.

○ **Reflection Activity:** Students write a reflection on how they can incorporate empathy into their leadership style and why it is important.

Week 2 Lesson Plans Day 1: Empathy in Different Cultures

Objective: Students will explore how empathy is expressed in different cultures
and understand the importance of cultural sensitivity.

Activities:

1. Cultural Exploration:

○ **Traditional:** Students research and present on how different cultures express empathy.

○ **VR:** Use VR experiences to immerse students in different cultural settings, observing and interacting with local customs and practices.

○ **Reflection Activity:** After the presentations or VR experiences, students write a reflection on what they learned about empathy in different cultures and how it can influence their own behavior.

2. Cultural Sensitivity Workshop:

○ **Traditional:** Conduct a workshop on cultural sensitivity and respectful communication.

○ **VR:** Create VR scenarios where students practice culturally sensitive interactions.

○ **Reflection Activity:** Students write a reflection on the importance of cultural sensitivity and how they can apply it in their daily interactions.

3. Group Discussion:

○ **Traditional:** Discuss the importance of understanding and respecting cultural differences.

○ **VR:** Host a virtual group discussion in a VR classroom setting, allowing students to share their insights.

○ **Reflection Activity:** Students write a reflection on what they learned from the discussion and how it can help them be more empathetic and inclusive.

Day 2: Empathy and Communication

Objective: Students will learn effective communication skills that enhance empathy.

Activities:

1. Non-Verbal Communication:

○ **Traditional:** Teach students about body language, facial expressions, and tone of voice.

○ **VR:** Use VR simulations to practice interpreting and using non-verbal communication.

○ **Reflection Activity:** Students write a reflection on how non-verbal communication affects their interactions and how they can improve their non-verbal cues.

2. Empathetic Communication Exercises:

○ **Traditional:** Role-play scenarios where students practice empathetic communication.

○ **VR:** Develop VR scenarios where students must communicate empathetically in various situations.

○ **Reflection Activity:** After the exercises, students write a reflection on the challenges and benefits of empathetic communication.

3. Feedback Session:

○ **Traditional:** Provide feedback on students' communication skills and areas for improvement.

○ **VR:** Use VR tools to give real-time feedback during simulations.

○ **Reflection Activity:** Students write a reflection on the feedback they received and how they plan to improve their communication skills.

Day 3: Empathy and Inclusion in the Workplace

Objective: Students will understand the role of empathy and inclusion in professional settings.

Activities:

1. Case Studies:

o **Traditional:** Analyze case studies of companies that successfully implement empathy and inclusion.

o **VR:** Create VR scenarios based on real-world case studies for students to explore.

o **Reflection Activity:** Students write a reflection on what they learned from the case studies and how they can apply these principles in their future careers.

2. Role-Playing:

o **Traditional:** Role-play workplace scenarios that require empathy and inclusion.

o **VR:** Use VR simulations to practice handling workplace situations with empathy.

o **Reflection Activity:** After the role-playing, students write a reflection on how empathy and inclusion can improve workplace dynamics.

3. Panel Discussion:

o **Traditional:** Invite professionals to discuss the importance of empathy and inclusion in their fields.

o **VR:** Host a virtual panel discussion with guest speakers in a VR environment.

○ **Reflection Activity:** Students write a reflection on the insights gained from the panel discussion and how they can incorporate empathy and inclusion into their professional lives.

Day 4: Empathy and Conflict Resolution

Objective: Students will learn techniques for resolving conflicts empathetically.

Activities:

1. Conflict Resolution Techniques:

○ **Traditional:** Teach techniques such as active listening, mediation, and finding common ground.

○ **VR:** Use VR modules to practice conflict resolution in simulated scenarios.

○ **Reflection Activity:** Students write a reflection on which conflict resolution techniques they found most effective and how they plan to use them.

2. Conflict Role-Playing:

○ **Traditional:** Role-play conflicts and practice resolving them using empathy.

○ **VR:** Develop VR scenarios where students must resolve conflicts empathetically.

○ **Reflection Activity:** After the role-playing, students write a reflection on the role of empathy in resolving conflicts and how it can be applied in real-life situations.

3. Reflection Session:

○ **Traditional:** Reflect on the role of empathy in resolving conflicts and share experiences.

○ **VR:** Use a VR journaling app to reflect on conflict resolution experiences.

○ **Reflection Activity:** Students write a reflection on their conflict resolution experiences and how they can improve their empathetic responses.

Day 5: Empathy and Inclusion in Community Building

Objective: Students will apply empathy and inclusion to build supportive communities.

Activities:

1. Community Projects:

o **Traditional:** Plan and execute community service projects that promote empathy and inclusion.

o **VR:** Use VR platforms to collaborate on virtual community projects.

o **Reflection Activity:** After the projects, students write a reflection on the impact of their work and how it promoted empathy and inclusion.

2. Building Supportive Networks:

o **Traditional:** Discuss the importance of supportive networks and how to build them.

o **VR:** Create VR scenarios where students practice building and maintaining supportive networks.

o **Reflection Activity:** Students write a reflection on the importance of supportive networks and how they can contribute to building them.

3. Celebration of Diversity:

o **Traditional:** Organize an event to celebrate the diversity within the community.

o **VR:** Host a virtual celebration in a VR environment, showcasing different cultures and experiences.

○ **Reflection Activity:** Students write a reflection on what they learned from the celebration and how it enhanced their understanding of diversity.

Week 3 Lesson Plans Day 1: Empathy and Storytelling

Objective: Students will use storytelling to understand and express empathy.

Activities:

1. Personal Stories:

○ **Traditional:** Students share personal stories that highlight moments of empathy.

○ **VR:** Use VR storytelling tools to create and share immersive personal stories.

○ **Reflection Activity:** After sharing their stories, students write a reflection on how telling and listening to these stories helped them understand and feel empathy.

2. Empathy Through Literature:

○ **Traditional:** Read and discuss stories or books that emphasize empathy.

○ **VR:** Explore VR adaptations of empathetic stories and discuss the experiences.

○ **Reflection Activity:** Students write a reflection on how the stories they read or experienced in VR changed their understanding of empathy.

3. Creative Writing:

○ **Traditional:** Students write their own stories focusing on empathy and inclusion.

○ **VR:** Use VR creative writing apps to craft and visualize their stories.

   ○ **Reflection Activity:** After writing their stories, students reflect on how creating a story about empathy influenced their own empathetic feelings and behaviors.

Day 2: Empathy in Digital Spaces

Objective: Students will learn about empathy in online interactions and digital citizenship.

Activities:

1. Digital Citizenship:

○ **Traditional:** Teach the principles of respectful and empathetic online behavior.

○ **VR:** Use VR simulations to practice digital citizenship in virtual communities.

○ **Reflection Activity:** Students write a reflection on the importance of empathy in digital interactions and how they can apply what they learned to their online behavior.

2. Online Empathy Exercises:

○ **Traditional:** Role-play online scenarios that require empathetic responses.

○ **VR:** Develop VR scenarios where students navigate online interactions with empathy.

○ **Reflection Activity:** After the exercises, students write a reflection on the challenges and benefits of showing empathy online.

3. Cyberbullying Awareness:

○ **Traditional:** Discuss the impact of cyberbullying and strategies to combat it.

○ **VR:** Create VR experiences that simulate the effects of cyberbullying and promote empathy.

○ **Reflection Activity:** Students write a reflection on how understanding the impact of cyberbullying has changed their perspective and how they can help prevent it.

Day 3: Empathy and Environmental Stewardship

Objective: Students will understand the connection between empathy and caring for the environment.

Activities:

1. Environmental Impact:

o **Traditional:** Discuss how empathy extends to caring for the environment and future generations.

o **VR:** Use VR experiences to explore the impact of environmental issues and solutions.

o **Reflection Activity:** Students write a reflection on how learning about environmental issues has influenced their sense of empathy towards the planet and future generations.

2. Eco-Friendly Projects:

o **Traditional:** Plan and execute projects that promote environmental stewardship.

o **VR:** Collaborate on virtual eco-friendly projects using VR platforms.

o **Reflection Activity:** After completing the projects, students write a reflection on the impact of their work and how it promoted environmental empathy.

3. Nature Walks:

o **Traditional:** Organize nature walks to connect with the environment and reflect on its importance.

o **VR:** Use VR nature experiences to explore different ecosystems and their significance.

○ **Reflection Activity:** Students write a reflection on how connecting with nature has deepened their empathy for the environment.

Day 4: Empathy and Historical Perspectives

Objective: Students will explore historical events through the lens of empathy.

Activities:

1. Historical Case Studies:

○ **Traditional:** Analyze historical events and figures that exemplify empathy.

○ **VR:** Use VR to experience historical events and understand the perspectives of those involved.

○ **Reflection Activity:** Students write a reflection on how studying historical empathy has changed their understanding of history and its impact.

2. Empathy in History:

○ **Traditional:** Discuss how empathy influenced key historical moments and movements.

○ **VR:** Create VR scenarios that allow students to step into the shoes of historical figures.

○ **Reflection Activity:** After the discussions or VR experiences, students write a reflection on how empathy shaped historical outcomes and what they learned from it.

3. Reflective Writing:

○ **Traditional:** Write reflections on how empathy shaped historical outcomes.

○ **VR:** Use VR journaling tools to reflect on historical empathy experiences.

○ **Reflection Activity:** Students write a reflection on how reflecting on historical empathy has influenced their own empathetic behaviors.

Day 5: Empathy and Global Citizenship

Objective: Students will understand their role as global citizens and the importance of empathy in a global context.

Activities:

1. Global Issues:

- **Traditional:** Discuss global issues and how empathy can drive positive change.
- **VR:** Use VR to explore global challenges and the efforts to address them.
- **Reflection Activity:** Students write a reflection on how learning about global issues has influenced their sense of global empathy and responsibility.

2. Cultural Exchange:

- **Traditional:** Organize cultural exchange activities to promote global understanding.
- **VR:** Create VR cultural exchange experiences where students interact with peers from different countries.
- **Reflection Activity:** After the cultural exchanges, students write a reflection on how interacting with peers from different cultures has enhanced their empathy and global understanding.

3. Global Projects:

- **Traditional:** Plan and execute projects that address global issues with empathy.
- **VR:** Collaborate on virtual global projects using VR platforms.
- **Reflection Activity:** After completing the projects, students write a reflection on the impact of their work and how it promoted global empathy and citizenship.

Week 4 Lesson Plans

Day 1: Empathy and Art

Objective: Students will explore how art can be a powerful medium for expressing and understanding empathy.

Activities:

1. Art and Emotion:

○ **Traditional:** Analyze artworks that convey strong emotions and discuss the feelings they evoke.

○ **VR:** Use VR art galleries to explore and interact with empathetic artworks.

○ **Reflection Activity:** Students write a reflection on how the artworks made them feel and how art can be used to express and understand emotions.

2. Creative Expression:

○ **Traditional:** Students create their own art pieces that express empathy and share their stories.

○ **VR:** Use VR art creation tools to design and present empathetic art in a virtual gallery.

○ **Reflection Activity:** After creating their art, students write a reflection on the process and how it helped them express empathy.

3. Art Reflection:

○ **Traditional:** Reflect on how art can foster empathy and understanding.

○ **VR:** Use VR journaling tools to reflect on the experience of creating and viewing empathetic art.

○ **Reflection Activity:** Students write a reflection on how engaging with art has influenced their understanding of empathy.

Day 2: Empathy and Music

Objective: Students will understand how music can evoke empathy and connect people.

Activities:

1. Music and Emotion:

○ **Traditional:** Listen to and analyze songs that convey empathy and discuss their impact.

○ **VR:** Use VR music experiences to immerse students in empathetic musical performances.

○ **Reflection Activity:** Students write a reflection on how the music made them feel and how it can be used to connect with others.

2. Songwriting:

○ **Traditional:** Students write and perform songs that express empathy and inclusion.

○ **VR:** Use VR music creation tools to compose and share empathetic songs.

○ **Reflection Activity:** After writing and performing their songs, students write a reflection on how the process helped them express and understand empathy.

3. Music Sharing:

○ **Traditional:** Organize a music sharing session where students present their empathetic songs.

○ **VR:** Host a virtual concert in a VR environment to showcase students' musical creations.

○ **Reflection Activity:** Students write a reflection on how sharing their music with others influenced their understanding of empathy.

Day 3: Empathy and Physical Activity

Objective: Students will explore how physical activities can promote empathy and teamwork.

Activities:

1. Team-Building Exercises:

○ **Traditional:** Engage in physical activities that require teamwork and empathy, such as trust falls and cooperative games.

○ **VR:** Use VR sports and team-building simulations to practice empathy and collaboration.

○ **Reflection Activity:** Students write a reflection on how the team-building exercises helped them understand and practice empathy.

2. Empathy in Sports:

○ **Traditional:** Discuss the role of empathy in sportsmanship and fair play.

○ **VR:** Create VR scenarios where students experience the importance of empathy in sports.

○ **Reflection Activity:** Students write a reflection on how empathy can improve sportsmanship and relationships in sports.

3. Reflection on Physical Activity:

○ **Traditional:** Reflect on how physical activities can build empathy and strengthen relationships.

○ **VR:** Use VR journaling tools to reflect on the experiences of empathy in physical activities.

○ **Reflection Activity:** Students write a reflection on how participating in physical activities has influenced their understanding of empathy.

Day 4: Empathy and Literature

Objective: Students will use literature to explore and understand empathy.

Activities:

1. Book Discussions:

○ **Traditional:** Read and discuss books that highlight themes of empathy and inclusion.

○ **VR:** Use VR book clubs to discuss empathetic literature in a virtual setting.

○ **Reflection Activity:** Students write a reflection on how the books they read influenced their understanding of empathy.

2. Character Analysis:

○ **Traditional:** Analyze characters in literature and their empathetic actions.

○ **VR:** Create VR scenarios where students can interact with characters and explore their perspectives.

○ **Reflection Activity:** Students write a reflection on how analyzing characters helped them understand empathy.

3. Creative Writing:

○ **Traditional:** Write stories or poems that focus on empathy and inclusion.

○ **VR:** Use VR creative writing tools to craft and share empathetic literary works.

○ **Reflection Activity:** After writing their stories or poems, students write a reflection on how the creative process helped them express and understand empathy.

Day 5: Empathy and Technology

Objective: Students will explore how technology can be used to promote empathy and inclusion.

Activities:

1. Tech for Good:

○ **Traditional:** Discuss how technology can be used to solve social issues and promote empathy.

○ **VR:** Use VR experiences to explore tech innovations that foster empathy and inclusion.

○ **Reflection Activity:** Students write a reflection on how technology can be used to promote empathy and what they learned from the discussion.

2. Empathy Apps:

○ **Traditional:** Introduce apps and digital tools designed to teach and promote empathy.

○ **VR:** Use VR empathy training apps to practice empathetic interactions.

○ **Reflection Activity:** Students write a reflection on how using empathy apps influenced their understanding and practice of empathy.

3. Tech Projects:

○ **Traditional:** Develop projects that use technology to address issues of empathy and inclusion.

○ **VR:** Collaborate on virtual tech projects using VR platforms to create empathetic solutions.

○ **Reflection Activity:** After completing the projects, students write a reflection on how their work with technology promoted empathy and inclusion.

Week 5 Lesson Plans Day 1: Empathy and Media Literacy

Objective: Students will learn to critically analyze media and understand its

impact on empathy and inclusion.

Activities:

1. Media Analysis:

○ **Traditional:** Analyze different media sources (news articles, advertisements, social media) for their portrayal of empathy and inclusion.

○ **VR:** Use VR to explore virtual newsrooms and media environments, analyzing content for empathy and bias.

○ **Reflection Activity:** Students write a reflection on how media influences their perceptions of empathy and inclusion, and how they can be more critical consumers of media.

2. Creating Empathetic Media:

○ **Traditional:** Students create their own media pieces (articles, videos, social media posts) that promote empathy and inclusion.

○ **VR:** Use VR media creation tools to produce and share empathetic content.

○ **Reflection Activity:** After creating their media pieces, students write a reflection on the process and how they can use media to promote empathy and inclusion.

3. Group Discussion:

○ **Traditional:** Discuss the role of media in shaping public perception and empathy.

○ **VR:** Host a virtual group discussion in a VR classroom setting, allowing students to share their insights.

○ **Reflection Activity:** Students write a reflection on what they learned from the discussion and how they can apply it to their media consumption and creation.

Day 2: Empathy and Social Justice

Objective: Students will explore the connection between empathy and social justice, and how they can advocate for change.

Activities:

1. **Social Justice Issues:**
   o **Traditional:** Discuss various social justice issues and the role of empathy in addressing them.
   o **VR:** Use VR experiences to explore social justice movements and their impact.
   o **Reflection Activity:** Students write a reflection on how empathy can drive social justice and what they learned from exploring these issues.

2. **Advocacy Projects:**

   o **Traditional:** Develop projects that advocate for social justice and promote empathy.
   o **VR:** Collaborate on virtual advocacy projects using VR platforms.
   o **Reflection Activity:** After completing their projects, students write a reflection on the impact of their advocacy work and how it promoted empathy and social justice.

3. **Guest Speaker:**

   o **Traditional:** Invite a social justice advocate to speak about their experiences and the importance of empathy.
   o **VR:** Host a virtual guest speaker session in a VR environment.
   o **Reflection Activity:** Students write a reflection on the insights gained from the guest speaker and how they can apply these lessons to their own lives.

Day 3: Empathy and Mental Health

Objective: Students will understand the importance of empathy in supporting mental health and well-being.

Activities:

1. Mental Health Awareness:

○ **Traditional:** Discuss common mental health issues and how empathy can support those affected.

○ **VR:** Use VR simulations to experience and understand mental health challenges.

○ **Reflection Activity:** Students write a reflection on how learning about mental health issues has influenced their understanding of empathy.

2. Support Strategies:

○ **Traditional:** Teach strategies for providing empathetic support to peers with mental health issues.

○ **VR:** Practice these strategies in VR scenarios designed to simulate real-life situations.

○ **Reflection Activity:** After practicing support strategies, students write a reflection on how they can use these strategies to support others.

3. Reflection Session:

○ **Traditional:** Reflect on the importance of empathy in mental health support and share personal experiences.

○ **VR:** Use VR journaling tools to reflect on mental health and empathy experiences.

    ○ **Reflection Activity:** Students write a reflection on their experiences and how they can continue to support mental health with empathy.

Day 4: Empathy and Conflict Resolution in Diverse Settings

Objective: Students will learn conflict resolution techniques that are sensitive to cultural and individual differences.

Activities:

1. Conflict Resolution Techniques:

○ **Traditional:** Teach techniques such as mediation, negotiation, and finding common ground.

○ **VR:** Use VR modules to practice conflict resolution in diverse cultural settings.

○ **Reflection Activity:** Students write a reflection on which conflict resolution techniques they found most effective and how they plan to use them.

2. Role-Playing:

○ **Traditional:** Role-play conflicts that involve cultural or individual differences and practice resolving them empathetically.

○ **VR:** Develop VR scenarios where students must resolve conflicts with cultural sensitivity.

○ **Reflection Activity:** After the role-playing, students write a reflection on how empathy and cultural sensitivity can improve conflict resolution.

3. Group Reflection:

○ **Traditional:** Reflect on the role of empathy in resolving conflicts and share experiences.

○ **VR:** Use a VR journaling app to reflect on conflict resolution experiences.

○ **Reflection Activity:** Students write a reflection on their conflict resolution experiences and how they can improve their empathetic responses.

Day 5: Empathy and Leadership

Objective: Students will explore the role of empathy in effective leadership and practice empathetic leadership skills.

Activities:

1. Leadership Qualities:

○ **Traditional:** Discuss the qualities of empathetic leaders and analyze examples of empathetic leadership.

○ **VR:** Use VR simulations to experience leadership scenarios and practice empathetic decision-making.

○ **Reflection Activity:** Students write a reflection on the qualities of empathetic leaders and how they can develop these qualities in themselves.

2. Leadership Role-Playing:

○ **Traditional:** Role-play leadership scenarios that require empathy and inclusion.

○ **VR:** Create VR scenarios where students take on leadership roles and make decisions based on empathy.

○ **Reflection Activity:** After the role-playing, students write a reflection on how empathy can improve their leadership skills.

3. Leadership Projects:

○ **Traditional:** Develop projects that demonstrate empathetic leadership in action.

○ **VR:** Collaborate on virtual leadership projects using VR platforms.

○ **Reflection Activity:** After completing the projects, students write a reflection on how their work demonstrated empathetic leadership and what they learned from the experience.

Week 6 Lesson Plans Day 1: Empathy and Community Service

Objective: Students will understand the importance of community service and

how empathy drives meaningful contributions.

Activities:

1. Community Needs Assessment:

○ **Traditional:** Research and identify the needs of the local community.

○ **VR:** Use VR to explore virtual communities and understand their needs.

○ **Reflection Activity:** Students write a reflection on what they learned about the community's needs and how empathy can guide their service efforts.

2. Service Project Planning:

○ **Traditional:** Plan a community service project that addresses identified needs.

○ **VR:** Collaborate on planning a virtual community service project using VR platforms.

○ **Reflection Activity:** After planning the project, students write a reflection on the role of empathy in the planning process and how it can enhance the impact of their service.

3. Reflection on Service:

○ **Traditional:** Reflect on the planning process and the role of empathy in community service.

○ **VR:** Use VR journaling tools to reflect on the experience of planning a service project.

○ **Reflection Activity:** Students write a reflection on how the planning process has influenced their understanding of empathy and community service.

Day 2: Empathy and Global Perspectives

Objective: Students will explore global issues and understand the importance of empathy in a global context.

Activities:

1. Global Issue Research:

○ **Traditional:** Research global issues such as poverty, climate change, and human rights.

○ **VR:** Use VR to explore global issues and their impact on different communities.

○ **Reflection Activity:** Students write a reflection on how learning about global issues has influenced their understanding of empathy and global citizenship.

2. Global Empathy Projects:

○ **Traditional:** Develop projects that address global issues with empathy.

○ **VR:** Collaborate on virtual global projects using VR platforms.

○ **Reflection Activity:** After completing their projects, students write a reflection on the impact of their work and how it promoted empathy and global understanding.

3. Cultural Exchange:

○ **Traditional:** Organize cultural exchange activities to promote global understanding.

○ **VR:** Create VR cultural exchange experiences where students interact with peers from different countries.

○ **Reflection Activity:** Students write a reflection on how interacting with peers from different cultures has enhanced their empathy and global perspective.

Day 3: Empathy and Technology Ethics

Objective: Students will explore the ethical implications of technology and the role of empathy in tech development.

Activities:

1. Tech Ethics Discussion:

○ **Traditional:** Discuss ethical issues in technology, such as privacy, AI, and digital divide.

○ **VR:** Use VR to explore ethical dilemmas in technology and discuss their implications.

○ **Reflection Activity:** Students write a reflection on how ethical issues in technology can be addressed with empathy and what they learned from the discussion.

2. Ethical Tech Projects:

○ **Traditional:** Develop projects that address ethical issues in technology with empathy.

○ **VR:** Collaborate on virtual tech projects using VR platforms to create ethical solutions.

○ **Reflection Activity:** After completing their projects, students write a reflection on how their work addressed ethical issues and promoted empathy in technology.

3. Guest Speaker:

○ **Traditional:** Invite a tech ethicist to speak about the importance of empathy in technology.

○ **VR:** Host a virtual guest speaker session in a VR environment.

○ **Reflection Activity:** Students write a reflection on the insights gained from the guest speaker and how they can apply these lessons to their understanding of technology ethics.

Day 4: Empathy and Environmental Advocacy

Objective: Students will understand the role of empathy in environmental advocacy and how they can contribute.

Activities:

1. Environmental Issues Research:

○ **Traditional:** Research environmental issues such as pollution, deforestation, and climate change.

○ **VR:** Use VR to explore environmental issues and their impact on different ecosystems.

○ **Reflection Activity:** Students write a reflection on how learning about environmental issues has influenced their understanding of empathy and environmental stewardship.

2. Advocacy Campaigns:

○ **Traditional:** Develop advocacy campaigns that promote environmental stewardship.

○ **VR:** Collaborate on virtual advocacy campaigns using VR platforms.

○ **Reflection Activity:** After completing their campaigns, students write a reflection on the impact of their advocacy work and how it promoted empathy for the environment.

3. Nature Reflection:

○ **Traditional:** Reflect on the importance of nature and how empathy can drive environmental action.

○ **VR:** Use VR nature experiences to reflect on the connection between empathy and environmental advocacy.

○ **Reflection Activity:** Students write a reflection on how connecting with nature has deepened their empathy for the environment and inspired them to take action.

Day 5: Empathy and Personal Growth

Objective: Students will explore how empathy contributes to personal growth and self-awareness.

Activities:

1. Self-Reflection:

○ **Traditional:** Reflect on personal experiences and how empathy has influenced their growth.

○ **VR:** Use VR journaling tools to reflect on personal growth and empathy experiences.

○ **Reflection Activity:** Students write a reflection on how empathy has shaped their personal growth and what they have learned about themselves.

2. Goal Setting:

○ **Traditional:** Set personal goals that incorporate empathy and inclusion.

○ **VR:** Use VR goal-setting tools to visualize and plan empathetic personal goals.

○ **Reflection Activity:** After setting their goals, students write a reflection on how incorporating empathy into their goals can help them achieve personal growth.

3. Peer Support:

○ **Traditional:** Create a peer support system where students can share their goals and support each other.

○ **VR:** Use VR platforms to create virtual peer support groups.

○ **Reflection Activity:** Students write a reflection on how supporting their peers and receiving support has influenced their understanding of empathy and personal growth.

Week 7 Lesson Plans Day 1: Empathy and Storytelling through Film

Objective: Students will explore how films can be used to understand and express
empathy.

Activities:

1. Film Analysis:

○ **Traditional:** Watch and analyze films that highlight themes of empathy and inclusion.

○ **VR:** Use VR to watch immersive films and discuss the empathetic elements.

○ **Reflection Activity:** Students write a reflection on how the films they watched influenced their understanding of empathy and inclusion.

2. Film Creation:

○ **Traditional:** Students create short films or video projects that express empathy.

○ **VR:** Use VR film creation tools to produce and share empathetic films.

○ **Reflection Activity:** After creating their films, students write a reflection on the process and how it helped them express and understand empathy.

3. Group Discussion:

○ **Traditional:** Discuss the impact of films on empathy and how they can inspire change.

○ **VR:** Host a virtual group discussion in a VR classroom setting, allowing students to share their insights.

○ **Reflection Activity:** Students write a reflection on what they learned from the discussion and how films can be a powerful tool for promoting empathy.

Day 2: Empathy and Social Media

Objective: Students will learn to use social media responsibly and empathetically.

Activities:

1. Social Media Analysis:

○ **Traditional:** Analyze social media posts and campaigns that promote empathy and inclusion.

○ **VR:** Use VR to explore social media environments and discuss their impact on empathy.

○ **Reflection Activity:** Students write a reflection on how social media can influence empathy and inclusion, and how they can be more responsible users.

2. Creating Empathetic Content:

○ **Traditional:** Students create social media posts or campaigns that promote empathy and inclusion.

○ **VR:** Use VR social media creation tools to produce and share empathetic content.

○ **Reflection Activity:** After creating their content, students write a reflection on the process and how they can use social media to promote empathy and inclusion.

3. Digital Citizenship:

○ **Traditional:** Teach the principles of respectful and empathetic online behavior.

○ **VR:** Use VR simulations to practice digital citizenship in virtual communities.

○ **Reflection Activity:** Students write a reflection on what they learned about digital citizenship and how they can apply it to their online interactions.

Day 3: Empathy and Literature Circles

Objective: Students will use literature circles to explore and discuss themes of empathy and inclusion.

Activities:

1. Book Selection:

○ **Traditional:** Select books that highlight themes of empathy and inclusion for literature circles.

○ **VR:** Use VR book clubs to discuss empathetic literature in a virtual setting.

○ **Reflection Activity:** Students write a reflection on how the books they read influenced their understanding of empathy and inclusion.

2. Literature Circle Discussions:

○ **Traditional:** Organize literature circles where students discuss the books and their themes.

○ **VR:** Host virtual literature circle discussions in a VR environment.

○ **Reflection Activity:** Students write a reflection on what they learned from the literature circle discussions and how it enhanced their understanding of empathy.

3. Creative Responses:

○ **Traditional:** Students create projects (art, writing, presentations) based on their literature circle discussions.

○ **VR:** Use VR creative tools to produce and share projects inspired by the literature.

○ **Reflection Activity:** After creating their projects, students write a reflection on how the creative process helped them express and understand empathy.

Day 4: Empathy and Peer Mediation

Objective: Students will learn peer mediation techniques to resolve conflicts empathetically.

Activities:

1. Mediation Training:

○ **Traditional:** Teach students the principles and techniques of peer mediation.

○ **VR:** Use VR modules to practice peer mediation in simulated scenarios.

○ **Reflection Activity:** Students write a reflection on what they learned about peer mediation and how they can use these techniques to resolve conflicts empathetically.

2. Role-Playing:

○ **Traditional:** Role-play conflicts and practice resolving them using peer mediation techniques.

○ **VR:** Develop VR scenarios where students must mediate conflicts empathetically.

○ **Reflection Activity:** After the role-playing, students write a reflection on how empathy can improve their conflict resolution skills.

3. Reflection Session:

○ **Traditional:** Reflect on the role of empathy in peer mediation and share experiences.

○ **VR:** Use VR journaling tools to reflect on mediation experiences.

○ **Reflection Activity:** Students write a reflection on their mediation experiences and how they can improve their empathetic responses.

Day 5: Empathy and Community Building

Objective: Students will apply empathy to build supportive and inclusive communities.

Activities:

1. Community Mapping:

○ **Traditional:** Map out the local community and identify areas where empathy and inclusion can be improved.

○ **VR:** Use VR to explore virtual communities and identify areas for improvement.

○ **Reflection Activity:** Students write a reflection on what they learned about their community and how empathy can guide their efforts to improve it.

2. Community Projects:

○ **Traditional:** Plan and execute projects that promote empathy and inclusion in the community.

○ **VR:** Collaborate on virtual community projects using VR platforms.

○ **Reflection Activity:** After completing their projects, students write a reflection on the impact of their work and how it promoted empathy and inclusion.

3. Celebration of Community:

○ **Traditional:** Organize an event to celebrate the diversity and inclusivity within the community.

○ **VR:** Host a virtual celebration in a VR environment, showcasing different cultures and experiences.

○ **Reflection Activity:** Students write a reflection on how celebrating diversity has enhanced their understanding of empathy and inclusion.

Week 8 Lesson Plans

Day 1: Empathy and Creative Writing

Objective: Students will use creative writing to explore and express empathy.

Activities:

1. Empathy Prompts:

○ **Traditional:** Provide writing prompts that encourage students to write from the perspective of someone else.

○ **VR:** Use VR creative writing tools to visualize and write stories from different perspectives.

2. Peer Review:

○ **Traditional:** Students share their stories with peers and provide empathetic feedback.

○ **VR:** Use VR platforms to share and review stories in a virtual writing workshop.

3. Reflection:

○ **Traditional:** Reflect on how writing from another perspective can enhance empathy.

○ **VR:** Use VR journaling tools to reflect on the creative writing experience.

Day 2: Empathy and Science

Objective: Students will explore the role of empathy in scientific research and innovation.

Activities:

1. Ethical Science:

○ **Traditional:** Discuss ethical considerations in scientific research and the importance of empathy.

○ **VR:** Use VR to explore ethical dilemmas in science and discuss their implications.

2. Empathy in Innovation:

○ **Traditional:** Analyze case studies of scientific innovations that were driven by empathy.

○ **VR:** Create VR scenarios where students can explore empathetic innovations.

3. Science Projects:

○ **Traditional:** Develop science projects that address social or environmental issues with empathy.

○ **VR:** Collaborate on virtual science projects using VR platforms.

Day 3: Empathy and Drama

Objective: Students will use drama and role-playing to understand and express empathy.

Activities:

1. Role-Playing:

○ **Traditional:** Engage in role-playing activities that require students to step into different characters' shoes.

○ **VR:** Use VR drama tools to create and participate in immersive role-playing scenarios.

2. Improvisation:

○ **Traditional:** Practice improvisation exercises that focus on empathetic responses.

○ **VR:** Use VR improvisation tools to create spontaneous empathetic interactions.

3. Performance Reflection:

○ **Traditional:** Reflect on the role-playing and improvisation experiences and their impact on empathy.

○ **VR:** Use VR journaling tools to reflect on the drama activities.

Day 4: Empathy and History

Objective: Students will explore historical events through the lens of empathy and understand their impact.

Activities:

1. Historical Analysis:

○ **Traditional:** Analyze historical events and figures that exemplify empathy.

○ **VR:** Use VR to experience historical events and understand the perspectives of those involved.

2. Empathy in History Projects:

○ **Traditional:** Develop projects that highlight the role of empathy in historical events.

○ **VR:** Create VR scenarios that allow students to step into the shoes of historical figures.

3. Reflective Writing:

○ **Traditional:** Write reflections on how empathy shaped historical outcomes.

○ **VR:** Use VR journaling tools to reflect on historical empathy experiences.

Day 5: Empathy and Peer Support

Objective: Students will learn how to provide empathetic support to their peers.

Activities:

1. Peer Support Training:

o **Traditional:** Teach students techniques for providing empathetic support to their peers.

o **VR:** Use VR modules to practice peer support in simulated scenarios.

2. Support Groups:

o **Traditional:** Create peer support groups where students can share their experiences and provide support.

o **VR:** Use VR platforms to create virtual peer support groups.

3. Reflection Session:

o **Traditional:** Reflect on the importance of peer support and share personal experiences.

o **VR:** Use VR journaling tools to reflect on peer support experiences.

Week 9 Lesson Plans

Day 1: Empathy and Cultural Heritage

Objective: Students will explore and appreciate different cultural heritages and understand their importance in fostering empathy.

Activities:

1. Cultural Heritage Research:

○ **Traditional:** Research and present on different cultural heritages and their significance.

○ **VR:** Use VR to explore virtual cultural heritage sites and learn about their history.

2. Cultural Exchange:

○ **Traditional:** Organize a cultural exchange day where students share aspects of their own heritage.

○ **VR:** Create VR cultural exchange experiences where students can virtually visit and learn about different cultures.

3. Case Study:

○ **Traditional:** Study the case of the Smithsonian Folklife Festival, which celebrates cultural heritage and promotes understanding.

○ **VR:** Use VR to explore a virtual version of the Smithsonian Folklife Festival and discuss its impact on cultural empathy.

4. Reflection:

○ **Traditional:** Reflect on the importance of understanding and respecting cultural heritage.

○ **VR:** Use VR journaling tools to reflect on the cultural heritage experiences.

Day 2: Empathy and Environmental Sustainability

Objective: Students will understand the connection between empathy and environmental sustainability.

Activities:

1. Sustainability Projects:

○ **Traditional:** Develop projects that promote environmental sustainability and empathy for future generations.

○ **VR:** Collaborate on virtual sustainability projects using VR platforms.

2. Eco-Friendly Practices:

○ **Traditional:** Discuss and implement eco-friendly practices in daily life.

○ **VR:** Use VR to simulate the impact of eco-friendly practices on the environment.

3. Case Study:

○ **Traditional:** Analyze the case of Greta Thunberg and the global climate strikes, focusing on how empathy drives environmental activism.

○ **VR:** Use VR to explore virtual climate strike events and discuss their impact.

4. Nature Reflection:

○ **Traditional:** Reflect on the importance of nature and how empathy can drive environmental action.

○ **VR:** Use VR nature experiences to reflect on the connection between empathy and environmental sustainability.

Day 3: Empathy and Health Care

Objective: Students will explore the role of empathy in health care and understand its impact on patient care.

Activities:

1. Health Care Scenarios:

○ **Traditional:** Role-play health care scenarios that require empathetic interactions.

○ **VR:** Use VR simulations to practice empathetic patient care in various health care settings.

2. Guest Speaker:

○ **Traditional:** Invite a healthcare professional to speak about the importance of empathy in their work.

○ **VR:** Host a virtual guest speaker session in a VR environment.

3. Case Study:

○ **Traditional:** Study the case of Dr. Paul Farmer and Partners In Health, focusing on how empathy drives global health initiatives.

○ **VR:** Use VR to explore virtual health care settings inspired by Partners In Health and discuss their impact.

4. Reflection Session:

○ **Traditional:** Reflect on the role of empathy in health care and share personal experiences.

○ **VR:** Use VR journaling tools to reflect on health care empathy experiences.

Day 4: Empathy and Conflict Resolution in Schools

Objective: Students will learn conflict resolution techniques to create a more empathetic and inclusive school environment.

Activities:

1. Conflict Resolution Training:

    ○ **Traditional:** Teach students techniques for resolving conflicts empathetically.

    ○ **VR:** Use VR modules to practice conflict resolution in school settings.

2. Role-Playing:

○ **Traditional:** Role-play school conflicts and practice resolving them using empathy.

    ○ **VR:** Develop VR scenarios where students must resolve school conflicts empathetically.

3. Case Study:

○ **Traditional:** Analyze the case of restorative justice programs in schools, focusing on how empathy can resolve conflicts.

    ○ **VR:** Use VR to simulate restorative justice circles and discuss their impact.

4. Group Reflection:

○ **Traditional:** Reflect on the role of empathy in resolving school conflicts and share experiences.

    ○ **VR:** Use VR journaling tools to reflect on conflict resolution experiences.

Day 5: Empathy, Global Citizenship, and Self-Compassion

Objective: Students will understand their role as global citizens, the importance of empathy in a global context, and the significance of self-compassion.

Activities:

1. Global Issues:

○ **Traditional:** Discuss global issues and how empathy can drive positive change.

○ **VR:** Use VR to explore global challenges and the efforts to address them.

2. Cultural Exchange:

○ **Traditional:** Organize cultural exchange activities to promote global understanding.

○ **VR:** Create VR cultural exchange experiences where students interact with peers from different countries.

3. Case Study:

○ **Traditional:** Study the case of Malala Yousafzai and her advocacy for girls' education, focusing on how empathy drives global citizenship.

○ **VR:** Use VR to explore virtual environments inspired by Malala's story and discuss their impact.

4. Self-Compassion Exercises:

○ **Traditional:** Teach students techniques for practicing self-compassion, such as positive self-talk and mindfulness.

○ **VR:** Use VR mindfulness and meditation apps to practice self-compassion exercises.

5. Global Projects:

○ **Traditional:** Plan and execute projects that address global issues with empathy.

○ **VR:** Collaborate on virtual global projects using VR platforms.

Week 10 Lesson Plans

Day 1: Empathy and Teamwork

Objective: Students will learn the importance of empathy in teamwork and collaboration.

Activities:

1. Team-Building Exercises:

- **Traditional:** Engage in team-building activities that require cooperation and empathy, such as trust falls and cooperative games.
- **VR:** Use VR sports and team-building simulations to practice empathy and collaboration.

2. Empathy in Group Projects:

- **Traditional:** Work on group projects that require students to practice empathy and effective communication.
- **VR:** Collaborate on virtual group projects using VR platforms.

3. Case Study:

- **Traditional:** Analyze the case of the Apollo 13 mission, focusing on how teamwork and empathy helped the crew overcome challenges.
- **VR:** Use VR to simulate the Apollo 13 mission and discuss the importance of empathy in teamwork.

4. Reflection:

- **Traditional:** Reflect on the team-building activities and their impact on empathy and collaboration.
- **VR:** Use VR journaling tools to reflect on teamwork experiences.

Day 2: Empathy and Art Therapy

Objective: Students will explore how art can be used as a therapeutic tool to express and understand emotions.

Activities:

1. Art Therapy Session:

○ **Traditional:** Conduct an art therapy session where students create art to express their emotions.

○ **VR:** Use VR art creation tools to design and share therapeutic art pieces.

2. Group Discussion:

○ **Traditional:** Discuss the therapeutic benefits of art and how it can foster empathy.

○ **VR:** Host a virtual group discussion in a VR classroom setting, allowing students to share their art and experiences.

3. Case Study:

○ **Traditional:** Study the case of The Art Therapy Project, focusing on how art therapy helps individuals heal and connect.

○ **VR:** Use VR to explore virtual art therapy sessions and discuss their impact.

4. Reflection:

○ **Traditional:** Reflect on the art therapy session and its impact on emotional expression and empathy.

○ **VR:** Use VR journaling tools to reflect on the art therapy experience.

Day 3: Empathy and Technology Design

Objective: Students will learn how empathy can be integrated into the design of technology and user experiences.

Activities:

1. User-Centered Design:

o **Traditional:** Teach the principles of user-centered design and how empathy plays a role.

o **VR:** Use VR design tools to create user-centered technology solutions.

2. Design Thinking Workshop:

o **Traditional:** Conduct a design thinking workshop where students develop empathetic tech solutions.

o **VR:** Collaborate on virtual design thinking projects using VR platforms.

3. Case Study:

o **Traditional:** Analyze the case of IDEO, focusing on how empathy-driven design leads to innovative solutions.

o **VR:** Use VR to explore IDEO's design process and discuss its impact.

4. Reflection:

o **Traditional:** Reflect on the design thinking workshop and the role of empathy in technology design.

o **VR:** Use VR journaling tools to reflect on the design experience.

Day 4: Empathy and Literature

Objective: Students will use literature to explore and understand empathy.

Activities:

1. Book Discussions:

    ○ **Traditional:** Read and discuss books that highlight themes of empathy and inclusion.

    ○ **VR:** Use VR book clubs to discuss empathetic literature in a virtual setting.

2. Character Analysis:

○ **Traditional:** Analyze characters in literature and their empathetic actions.

    ○ **VR:** Create VR scenarios where students can interact with characters and explore their perspectives.

3. Case Study:

○ **Traditional:** Study the case of "To Kill a Mockingbird" by Harper Lee, focusing on how empathy is portrayed through the characters.

    ○ **VR:** Use VR to explore scenes from "To Kill a Mockingbird" and discuss their impact.

4. Creative Writing:

○ **Traditional:** Write stories or poems that focus on empathy and inclusion.

    ○ **VR:** Use VR creative writing tools to craft and share empathetic literary works.

Day 5: Empathy and Mindfulness

Objective: Students will explore the connection between empathy and mindfulness and practice mindfulness techniques.

Activities:

1. Mindfulness Exercises:

○ **Traditional:** Teach mindfulness exercises such as deep breathing, meditation, and body scans.

○ **VR:** Use VR mindfulness and meditation apps to practice these techniques.

2. Mindful Listening:

○ **Traditional:** Practice mindful listening exercises where students focus on listening without judgment.

○ **VR:** Use VR simulations to practice mindful listening in various scenarios.

3. Case Study:

○ **Traditional:** Study the case of Jon Kabat-Zinn and the development of Mindfulness-Based Stress Reduction (MBSR), focusing on how mindfulness fosters empathy.

○ **VR:** Use VR to explore MBSR practices and discuss their impact.

4. Reflection:

○ **Traditional:** Reflect on the mindfulness exercises and their impact on empathy and self-awareness.

○ **VR:** Use VR journaling tools to reflect on the mindfulness experience.

Week 11 Lesson Plans

Day 1: Self-Awareness and Emotional Intelligence

Objective: Students will develop self-awareness and understand its role in emotional intelligence.

Activities:

1. Mindful Observation:

o **Traditional:** Practice mindful observation exercises where students focus on their thoughts and feelings without judgment.

o **VR:** Use VR mindfulness apps to guide students through mindful observation exercises.

2. Emotional Journaling:

o **Traditional:** Keep a daily journal where students reflect on their emotions and triggers.

o **VR:** Use VR journaling tools to document and reflect on emotional experiences.

3. Case Study:

o **Traditional:** Study the case of Daniel Goleman's work on emotional intelligence, focusing on the importance of self-awareness.

o **VR:** Use VR to explore scenarios that highlight self-awareness and discuss their impact.

4. Reflection:

o **Traditional:** Reflect on the mindful observation and journaling exercises and their impact on self-awareness.

o **VR:** Use VR journaling tools to reflect on the self-awareness activities.

Day 2: Self-Regulation and Emotional Intelligence

Objective: Students will learn techniques for self-regulation and understand its importance in emotional intelligence.

Activities:

1. Breathing Exercises:

○ **Traditional:** Practice deep breathing exercises to help manage emotions.

○ **VR:** Use VR breathing exercises apps to guide students through relaxation techniques.

2. Impulse Control Activities:

○ **Traditional:** Engage in activities that require impulse control, such as delayed gratification exercises.

○ **VR:** Use VR simulations to practice impulse control in various scenarios.

3. Case Study:

○ **Traditional:** Study the case of Marshmallow Test by Walter Mischel, focusing on the importance of self-regulation.

○ **VR:** Use VR to simulate the Marshmallow Test and discuss its findings.

4. Reflection:

○ **Traditional:** Reflect on the breathing exercises and impulse control activities and their impact on self-regulation.

○ **VR:** Use VR journaling tools to reflect on the self-regulation activities.

Day 3: Empathy and Emotional Intelligence

Objective: Students will explore the connection between empathy and emotional intelligence.

Activities:

1. Role-Playing Scenarios:

○ **Traditional:** Engage in role-playing activities that require students to practice empathy.

○ **VR:** Use VR role-playing tools to create and participate in empathetic scenarios.

2. Empathy Mapping:

○ **Traditional:** Create empathy maps to understand others' perspectives and emotions.

○ **VR:** Use VR tools to create digital empathy maps and explore different perspectives.

3. Case Study:

○ **Traditional:** Study the case of the Empathy Museum, focusing on how empathy can be cultivated through experiences.

○ **VR:** Use VR to explore virtual exhibits of the Empathy Museum and discuss their impact.

4. Reflection:

○ **Traditional:** Reflect on the role-playing and empathy mapping activities and their impact on understanding others.

○ **VR:** Use VR journaling tools to reflect on the empathy activities.

Day 4: Social Skills and Emotional Intelligence

Objective: Students will develop social skills that enhance emotional intelligence.

Activities:

1. Active Listening Exercises:

○ **Traditional:** Practice active listening exercises where students focus on listening without interrupting.

○ **VR:** Use VR simulations to practice active listening in various scenarios.

2. Communication Skills Workshop:

○ **Traditional:** Conduct a workshop on effective communication skills, including non-verbal cues and assertiveness.

○ **VR:** Use VR tools to practice and refine communication skills in simulated environments.

3. Case Study:

○ **Traditional:** Study the case of Dale Carnegie's principles from "How to Win Friends and Influence People," focusing on social skills.

○ **VR:** Use VR to explore scenarios inspired by Carnegie's principles and discuss their impact.

4. Reflection:

○ **Traditional:** Reflect on the active listening and communication skills exercises and their impact on social interactions.

○ **VR:** Use VR journaling tools to reflect on the social skills activities.

Day 5: Self-Compassion and Emotional Intelligence

Objective: Students will understand the importance of self-compassion in emotional intelligence and practice self-compassion techniques.

Activities:

1. Self-Compassion Exercises:

○ **Traditional:** Teach students techniques for practicing self-compassion, such as positive self-talk and mindfulness.

○ **VR:** Use VR mindfulness and meditation apps to practice self-compassion exercises.

2. Kindness Journaling:

○ **Traditional:** Keep a kindness journal where students document acts of kindness towards themselves and others.

○ **VR:** Use VR journaling tools to document and reflect on acts of kindness.

3. Case Study:

○ **Traditional:** Study the case of Kristin Neff's work on self-compassion, focusing on its role in emotional intelligence.

○ **VR:** Use VR to explore scenarios inspired by Neff's research and discuss their impact.

4. Reflection:

○ **Traditional:** Reflect on the self-compassion exercises and their impact on emotional well-being.

○ **VR:** Use VR journaling tools to reflect on the self-compassion activities.

Week 12 Lesson Plans

Day 1: Self-Expression through Movement

Objective: Students will explore how movement can be used as a form of self-expression and emotional release.

Activities:

1. Movement Exploration:

o **Traditional:** Engage in free-form movement exercises where students express their emotions through dance.

o **VR:** Use VR dance apps to explore different styles of movement and express emotions.

2. Emotion Dance:

o **Traditional:** Create dances that represent different emotions (e.g., joy, sadness, anger).

o **VR:** Use VR to create and share dances that express various emotions.

3. Case Study:

o **Traditional:** Study the case of the "Dance Your PhD" contest, focusing on how scientists use dance to express complex ideas.

o **VR:** Use VR to explore winning entries from the "Dance Your PhD" contest and discuss their impact.

4. Reflection:

o **Traditional:** Reflect on the movement exercises and their impact on emotional expression.

o **VR:** Use VR journaling tools to reflect on the dance activities.

Day 2: Dance and Emotional Intelligence

Objective: Students will understand how dance can enhance emotional intelligence and self-awareness.

Activities:

1. Dance and Emotions:

○ **Traditional:** Discuss how different dance styles can convey various emotions.

○ **VR:** Use VR dance experiences to explore how different movements express emotions.

2. Choreography Creation:

○ **Traditional:** Create a dance routine that tells a story through emotional expression.

○ **VR:** Use VR choreography tools to design and share a dance routine.

3. Case Study:

○ **Traditional:** Study the case of Alvin Ailey's "Revelations," focusing on how dance can convey powerful emotional narratives.

○ **VR:** Use VR to explore a virtual performance of "Revelations" and discuss its emotional impact.

4. Reflection:

○ **Traditional:** Reflect on the dance and emotional intelligence activities and their impact on self-awareness.

○ **VR:** Use VR journaling tools to reflect on the dance experiences.

Day 3: Movement and Mindfulness

Objective: Students will explore the connection between movement, mindfulness, and emotional well-being.

Activities:

1. Mindful Movement:

○ **Traditional:** Practice mindful movement exercises such as yoga or tai chi.

○ **VR:** Use VR mindfulness apps to guide students through mindful movement practices.

2. Dance Meditation:

○ **Traditional:** Engage in dance meditation where students move freely to music, focusing on the present moment.

○ **VR:** Use VR dance meditation apps to facilitate a mindful dance experience.

3. Case Study:

○ **Traditional:** Study the case of Gabrielle Roth's 5Rhythms, focusing on how movement can be a form of meditation and self-discovery.

○ **VR:** Use VR to explore a virtual 5Rhythms session and discuss its impact.

4. Reflection:

○ **Traditional:** Reflect on the mindful movement and dance meditation activities and their impact on emotional well-being.

○ **VR:** Use VR journaling tools to reflect on the mindfulness experiences.

Day 4: Dance and Cultural Expression

Objective: Students will explore how dance can be used to express cultural identity and foster empathy.

Activities:

1. Cultural Dance Exploration:

○ **Traditional:** Research and learn dances from different cultures.

○ **VR:** Use VR to explore and learn cultural dances from around the world.

2. Cultural Dance Performance:

○ **Traditional:** Perform a cultural dance and discuss its significance.

○ **VR:** Use VR to create and share a virtual performance of a cultural dance.

3. Case Study:

○ **Traditional:** Study the case of the National Dance Institute, focusing on how dance programs can promote cultural understanding and empathy.

○ **VR:** Use VR to explore virtual performances by the National Dance Institute and discuss their impact.

4. Reflection:

○ **Traditional:** Reflect on the cultural dance activities and their impact on empathy and cultural understanding.

○ **VR:** Use VR journaling tools to reflect on the cultural dance experiences.

Day 5: Dance and Self-Compassion

Objective: Students will understand the importance of self-compassion and use dance as a tool for self-care.

Activities:

1. Self-Compassion Dance:

○ **Traditional:** Create a dance routine that focuses on self-compassion and self-care.

○ **VR:** Use VR dance tools to design and share a self-compassion dance routine.

2. Dance Reflection:

○ **Traditional:** Reflect on how dance can be used as a form of self-care and emotional release.

○ **VR:** Use VR journaling tools to reflect on the self-compassion dance activities.

3. Case Study:

○ **Traditional:** Study the case of Dance Movement Therapy, focusing on how dance can be used for emotional healing and self-compassion.

○ **VR:** Use VR to explore virtual Dance Movement Therapy sessions and discuss their impact.

4. Reflection:

○ **Traditional:** Reflect on the self-compassion dance activities and their impact on emotional well-being.

○ **VR:** Use VR journaling tools to reflect on the self-compassion experiences.

Week 13 Lesson Plans

Day 1: Introduction to Dance as Storytelling

Objective: Students will understand the basics of how dance can be used to tell stories.

Activities:

1. Dance and Narrative:

o **Traditional:** Discuss how different dance styles can convey stories and emotions.

o **VR:** Use VR dance experiences to explore how movement can tell a story.

2. Storytelling through Movement:

o **Traditional:** Practice basic dance movements that represent different emotions and actions.

o **VR:** Use VR dance tools to create and share movements that tell a story.

3. Case Study:

o

Traditional: Study the case of Kathak, a classical Indian dance[1]

---

1. https://www.kalashriacademy.com/kathak-art-of-storytelling/

2. https://www.kalashriacademy.com/kathak-art-of-storytelling/

3. https://www.kalashriacademy.com/kathak-art-of-storytelling/

4. https://www.kalashriacademy.com/kathak-art-of-storytelling/

5. https://www.kalashriacademy.com/kathak-art-of-storytelling/

6. https://www.kalashriacademy.com/kathak-art-of-storytelling/

7. https://www.kalashriacademy.com/kathak-art-of-storytelling/

8. https://www.kalashriacademy.com/kathak-art-of-storytelling/

9. https://www.kalashriacademy.com/kathak-art-of-storytelling/

[0]form[11]

known[12]for[13]its[14]storytelling[15]through[16]intricate[17]footwork,[18]hand[2][0]gestures,[20] and[21]facial[22]expressions[23][24].

○ **VR:** Use VR to explore a virtual Kathak performance and discuss its storytelling elements.

4. Reflection:

○ **Traditional:** Reflect on the dance and narrative activities and their impact on understanding storytelling through movement.

○ **VR:** Use VR journaling tools to reflect on the storytelling dance experiences.

Day 2: Choreography and Storytelling

Objective: Students will learn how to create choreography that tells a story.

10. https://www.kalashriacademy.com/kathak-art-of-storytelling/

11. https://www.kalashriacademy.com/kathak-art-of-storytelling/

12. https://www.kalashriacademy.com/kathak-art-of-storytelling/

13. https://www.kalashriacademy.com/kathak-art-of-storytelling/

14. https://www.kalashriacademy.com/kathak-art-of-storytelling/

15. https://www.kalashriacademy.com/kathak-art-of-storytelling/

16. https://www.kalashriacademy.com/kathak-art-of-storytelling/

17. https://www.kalashriacademy.com/kathak-art-of-storytelling/

18. https://www.kalashriacademy.com/kathak-art-of-storytelling/

19. https://www.kalashriacademy.com/kathak-art-of-storytelling/

20. https://www.kalashriacademy.com/kathak-art-of-storytelling/

21. https://www.kalashriacademy.com/kathak-art-of-storytelling/

22. https://www.kalashriacademy.com/kathak-art-of-storytelling/

23. https://www.kalashriacademy.com/kathak-art-of-storytelling/

24. https://www.kalashriacademy.com/kathak-art-of-storytelling/

Activities:

1. Choreography Basics:

○ **Traditional:** Teach the basics of choreography and how to structure a dance narrative.

○ **VR:** Use VR choreography tools to design and share dance routines.

2. Creating a Dance Story:

○ **Traditional:** Work in groups to create a short dance piece that tells a story.

○ **VR:** Collaborate on virtual dance projects using VR platforms.

3. Case Study:

○

Traditional:[25]Study[26]the[27]case[28]of[29]Alvin[30]Ailey's[31]"Revelations,"[32]focusing[33]on[34]

how[35]choreography[36]can[37]convey[38]powerful[39]narratives[40][41].

25. https://www.kalashriacademy.com/kathak-art-of-storytelling/

26. https://www.kalashriacademy.com/kathak-art-of-storytelling/

27. https://www.kalashriacademy.com/kathak-art-of-storytelling/

28. https://www.kalashriacademy.com/kathak-art-of-storytelling/

29. https://www.kalashriacademy.com/kathak-art-of-storytelling/

30. https://www.kalashriacademy.com/kathak-art-of-storytelling/

31. https://www.kalashriacademy.com/kathak-art-of-storytelling/

32. https://www.kalashriacademy.com/kathak-art-of-storytelling/

33. https://www.kalashriacademy.com/kathak-art-of-storytelling/

34. https://www.kalashriacademy.com/kathak-art-of-storytelling/

35. https://www.kalashriacademy.com/kathak-art-of-storytelling/

36. https://www.kalashriacademy.com/kathak-art-of-storytelling/

37. https://www.kalashriacademy.com/kathak-art-of-storytelling/

38. https://www.kalashriacademy.com/kathak-art-of-storytelling/

○ **VR:** Use VR to explore a virtual performance of "Revelations" and discuss its storytelling elements.

4. Reflection:

○ **Traditional:** Reflect on the choreography and storytelling activities and their impact on understanding dance as a narrative form.

○ **VR:** Use VR journaling tools to reflect on the choreography experiences.

Day 3: Dance and Cultural Stories

Objective: Students will explore how different cultures use dance to tell stories.

Activities:

1. Cultural Dance Research:

○ **Traditional:** Research and present on different cultural dances and their storytelling elements.

○ **VR:** Use VR to explore and learn cultural dances from around the world.

2. Cultural Dance Performance:

○ **Traditional:** Perform a cultural dance and discuss its significance and story.

○ **VR:** Use VR to create and share a virtual performance of a cultural dance.

---

39. https://www.kalashriacademy.com/kathak-art-of-storytelling/

40. https://www.kalashriacademy.com/kathak-art-of-storytelling/

41. https://www.demodemagazine.com/dance-as-a-narrative-conveying-stories-through-movement-de-mode-global

3. Case Study:

○

Traditional:[42]Study[43]the[44]case[45]of[46]traditional[47]folk[48]dances,[49]focusing[50]on[51] how they convey cultural stories and heritage[52][53].

○ **VR:** Use VR to explore virtual performances of traditional folk dances and discuss their storytelling elements.

4. Reflection:

○ **Traditional:** Reflect on the cultural dance activities and their impact on understanding cultural stories through dance.

○ **VR:** Use VR journaling tools to reflect on the cultural dance experiences.

Day 4: Dance and Personal Stories

Objective: Students will use dance to express their own personal stories and experiences.

Activities:

1. Personal Story Exploration:

42. https://www.kalashriacademy.com/kathak-art-of-storytelling/

43. https://www.kalashriacademy.com/kathak-art-of-storytelling/

44. https://www.kalashriacademy.com/kathak-art-of-storytelling/

45. https://www.kalashriacademy.com/kathak-art-of-storytelling/

46. https://www.kalashriacademy.com/kathak-art-of-storytelling/

47. https://www.kalashriacademy.com/kathak-art-of-storytelling/

48. https://www.kalashriacademy.com/kathak-art-of-storytelling/

49. https://www.kalashriacademy.com/kathak-art-of-storytelling/

50. https://www.kalashriacademy.com/kathak-art-of-storytelling/

51. https://www.kalashriacademy.com/kathak-art-of-storytelling/

52. https://www.kalashriacademy.com/kathak-art-of-storytelling/

53. https://westendinschools.org.uk/blog/storytelling-in-dance

○ **Traditional:** Reflect on personal experiences and emotions that can be expressed through dance.

○ **VR:** Use VR journaling tools to document personal stories and emotions.

2. Creating a Personal Dance:

○ **Traditional:** Create a dance piece that tells a personal story or experience.

○ **VR:** Use VR dance tools to design and share a personal dance routine.

3. Case Study:

○

Traditional:[54]Study[55]the[56]case[57]of[58]contemporary[59]dance[60]pieces[61]that [62]focus[63]

on[64]personal[65]narratives,[66]such[67]as[68]works[69]by[70]Pina[71]Bausch[72][73].

---

54. https://www.kalashriacademy.com/kathak-art-of-storytelling/

55. https://www.kalashriacademy.com/kathak-art-of-storytelling/

56. https://www.kalashriacademy.com/kathak-art-of-storytelling/

57. https://www.kalashriacademy.com/kathak-art-of-storytelling/

58. https://www.kalashriacademy.com/kathak-art-of-storytelling/

59. https://www.kalashriacademy.com/kathak-art-of-storytelling/

60. https://www.kalashriacademy.com/kathak-art-of-storytelling/

61. https://www.kalashriacademy.com/kathak-art-of-storytelling/

62. https://www.kalashriacademy.com/kathak-art-of-storytelling/

63. https://www.kalashriacademy.com/kathak-art-of-storytelling/

64. https://www.kalashriacademy.com/kathak-art-of-storytelling/

65. https://www.kalashriacademy.com/kathak-art-of-storytelling/

66. https://www.kalashriacademy.com/kathak-art-of-storytelling/

67. https://www.kalashriacademy.com/kathak-art-of-storytelling/

68. https://www.kalashriacademy.com/kathak-art-of-storytelling/

69. https://www.kalashriacademy.com/kathak-art-of-storytelling/

○ **VR:** Use VR to explore virtual performances of contemporary dance pieces and discuss their personal storytelling elements.

4. Reflection:

○ **Traditional:** Reflect on the personal dance activities and their impact on self-expression and emotional release.

○ **VR:** Use VR journaling tools to reflect on the personal dance experiences.

Day 5: Dance, Empathy, and Storytelling

Objective: Students will understand how dance can foster empathy through storytelling.

Activities:

1. Empathy through Dance:

○ **Traditional:** Discuss how dance can create empathy by telling stories that resonate with others.

○ **VR:** Use VR dance experiences to explore how movement can evoke empathy.

2. Group Dance Project:

○ **Traditional:** Work in groups to create a dance piece that tells a story aimed at fostering empathy.

○ **VR:** Collaborate on virtual dance projects using VR platforms.

---

70. https://www.kalashriacademy.com/kathak-art-of-storytelling/

71. https://www.kalashriacademy.com/kathak-art-of-storytelling/

72. https://www.kalashriacademy.com/kathak-art-of-storytelling/

73. https://www.demodemagazine.com/dance-as-a-narrative-conveying-stories-through-movement-de-mode-global

3. Case Study:

○

Traditional:[74]Study[75]the[76]case[77]of[78]the[79]Empathy[80]Museum's[81]"A [8]
[2]Mile[83]in[84]My[85]
Shoes"[86]project,[87]focusing[88]on[89]how[90]storytelling[91]can[92]foster[9]
[6]empathy[94][295].

    ○ **VR:** Use VR to explore virtual exhibits of the Empathy Museum and discuss their impact.

---

74. https://www.kalashriacademy.com/kathak-art-of-storytelling/

75. https://www.kalashriacademy.com/kathak-art-of-storytelling/

76. https://www.kalashriacademy.com/kathak-art-of-storytelling/

77. https://www.kalashriacademy.com/kathak-art-of-storytelling/

78. https://www.kalashriacademy.com/kathak-art-of-storytelling/

79. https://www.kalashriacademy.com/kathak-art-of-storytelling/

80. https://www.kalashriacademy.com/kathak-art-of-storytelling/

81. https://www.kalashriacademy.com/kathak-art-of-storytelling/

82. https://www.kalashriacademy.com/kathak-art-of-storytelling/

83. https://www.kalashriacademy.com/kathak-art-of-storytelling/

84. https://www.kalashriacademy.com/kathak-art-of-storytelling/

85. https://www.kalashriacademy.com/kathak-art-of-storytelling/

86. https://www.kalashriacademy.com/kathak-art-of-storytelling/

87. https://www.kalashriacademy.com/kathak-art-of-storytelling/

88. https://www.kalashriacademy.com/kathak-art-of-storytelling/

89. https://www.kalashriacademy.com/kathak-art-of-storytelling/

90. https://www.kalashriacademy.com/kathak-art-of-storytelling/

91. https://www.kalashriacademy.com/kathak-art-of-storytelling/

92. https://www.kalashriacademy.com/kathak-art-of-storytelling/

93. https://www.kalashriacademy.com/kathak-art-of-storytelling/

94. https://www.kalashriacademy.com/kathak-art-of-storytelling/

95. https://www.demodemagazine.com/dance-as-a-narrative-conveying-stories-through-movement-de-mode-global

4. Reflection:

○ **Traditional:** Reflect on the group dance project and its impact on understanding empathy through storytelling.

○ **VR:** Use VR journaling tools to reflect on the empathy dance experiences.

Week 14 Lesson Plans

Day 1: Dance and Historical Narratives

Objective: Students will explore how dance can be used to tell historical stories and understand their significance.

Activities:

1. Historical Dance Research:

o **Traditional:** Research and present on historical events that have been depicted through dance.

o **VR:** Use VR to explore virtual performances of historical dance pieces.

2. Creating a Historical Dance:

o **Traditional:** Work in groups to create a dance piece that tells the story of a historical event.

o **VR:** Collaborate on virtual dance projects using VR platforms to depict historical narratives.

3. Case Study:

o **Traditional:** Study the case of Martha Graham's "Chronicle," focusing on how it depicts the impact of war and social issues.

o **VR:** Use VR to explore a virtual performance of "Chronicle" and discuss its historical storytelling elements.

4. Reflection:

o **Traditional:** Reflect on the historical dance activities and their impact on understanding history through movement.

o **VR:** Use VR journaling tools to reflect on the historical dance experiences.

Day 2: Dance and Social Justice

Objective: Students will understand how dance can be used to advocate for social justice and create awareness.

Activities:

1. Social Justice Dance Exploration:

○ **Traditional:** Discuss how dance has been used to address social justice issues.

○ **VR:** Use VR to explore virtual performances that focus on social justice themes.

2. Creating a Social Justice Dance:

○ **Traditional:** Create a dance piece that addresses a social justice issue.

○ **VR:** Use VR dance tools to design and share a social justice dance routine.

3. Case Study:

○ **Traditional:** Study the case of Bill T. Jones' "Still/Here," focusing on how it addresses themes of illness and survival.

○ **VR:** Use VR to explore a virtual performance of "Still/Here" and discuss its social justice elements.

4. Reflection:

○ **Traditional:** Reflect on the social justice dance activities and their impact on understanding and advocating for social issues.

○ **VR:** Use VR journaling tools to reflect on the social justice dance experiences.

Day 3: Dance and Community Stories

Objective: Students will explore how dance can be used to tell stories from their own communities and foster a sense of belonging.

Activities:

1. Community Dance Research:

    ○ **Traditional:** Research and present on dance traditions within their own communities.

    ○ **VR:** Use VR to explore virtual performances of community dance traditions.

2. Creating a Community Dance:

○ **Traditional:** Work in groups to create a dance piece that tells a story from their community.

    ○ **VR:** Collaborate on virtual dance projects using VR platforms to depict community narratives.

3. Case Study:

○ **Traditional:** Study the case of Urban Bush Women, focusing on how they use dance to tell stories of the African American community.

    ○ **VR:** Use VR to explore virtual performances by Urban Bush Women and discuss their community storytelling elements.

4. Reflection:

○ **Traditional:** Reflect on the community dance activities and their impact on understanding and celebrating community stories.

    ○ **VR:** Use VR journaling tools to reflect on the community dance experiences.

Day 4: Dance and Personal Growth

Objective: Students will use dance to explore personal growth and self-discovery.

Activities:

1. Personal Growth Exploration:

○ **Traditional:** Reflect on personal experiences of growth and how they can be expressed through dance.

○ **VR:** Use VR journaling tools to document personal growth stories and emotions.

2. Creating a Personal Growth Dance:

○ **Traditional:** Create a dance piece that represents a personal journey of growth and self-discovery.

○ **VR:** Use VR dance tools to design and share a personal growth dance routine.

3. Case Study:

○ **Traditional:** Study the case of Ohad Naharin's "Echad Mi Yodea," focusing on how it explores themes of identity and transformation.

○ **VR:** Use VR to explore a virtual performance of "Echad Mi Yodea" and discuss its personal growth elements.

4. Reflection:

○ **Traditional:** Reflect on the personal growth dance activities and their impact on self-discovery and emotional expression.

○ **VR:** Use VR journaling tools to reflect on the personal growth dance experiences.

Day 5: Dance and Empathy Building

Objective: Students will understand how dance can be used to build empathy and connect with others.

Activities:

1. Empathy Dance Exploration:
○ **Traditional:** Discuss how dance can create empathy by telling stories that resonate with others.

○ **VR:** Use VR dance experiences to explore how movement can evoke empathy.

2. Group Empathy Dance Project:

○ **Traditional:** Work in groups to create a dance piece that tells a story aimed at fostering empathy.

○ **VR:** Collaborate on virtual dance projects using VR platforms.

3. Case Study:

○ **Traditional:** Study the case of the Empathy Museum's "A Mile in My Shoes" project, focusing on how storytelling can foster empathy.

○ **VR:** Use VR to explore virtual exhibits of the Empathy Museum and discuss their impact.

4. Reflection:

○ **Traditional:** Reflect on the group empathy dance project and its impact on understanding empathy through storytelling.

○ **VR:** Use VR journaling tools to reflect on the empathy dance experiences.

Week 15 Lesson Plans

Day 1: Dance and Emotional Expression

Objective: Students will explore how dance can be used to express a wide range of emotions.

Activities:

1. Emotion Exploration:

    ○ **Traditional:** Practice dance movements that represent different emotions (e.g., joy, sadness, anger).

    ○ **VR:** Use VR dance tools to create and share movements that express various emotions.

2. Emotion Dance Creation:

○ **Traditional:** Create a short dance piece that focuses on expressing a specific emotion.

    ○ **VR:** Collaborate on virtual dance projects using VR platforms to depict emotional narratives.

3. Case Study:

○ **Traditional:** Study the case of Martha Graham's "Lamentation," focusing on how it conveys deep emotional expression.

    ○ **VR:** Use VR to explore a virtual performance of "Lamentation" and discuss its emotional storytelling elements.

4. Reflection:

○ **Traditional:** Reflect on the emotion dance activities and their impact on understanding and expressing emotions through movement.

    ○ **VR:** Use VR journaling tools to reflect on the emotional dance experiences.

Day 2: Dance and Resilience

Objective: Students will understand how dance can be used to build resilience and cope with challenges.

Activities:

1. Resilience through Movement:

○ **Traditional:** Discuss how dance can help build resilience and cope with stress.

○ **VR:** Use VR dance experiences to explore how movement can foster resilience.

2. Creating a Resilience Dance:

○ **Traditional:** Create a dance piece that represents overcoming challenges and building resilience.

○ **VR:** Use VR dance tools to design and share a resilience dance routine.

3. Case Study:

○ **Traditional:** Study the case of Misty Copeland, focusing on her journey and how dance helped her overcome obstacles.

○ **VR:** Use VR to explore virtual performances by Misty Copeland and discuss her resilience.

4. Reflection:

○ **Traditional:** Reflect on the resilience dance activities and their impact on understanding and building resilience through movement.

○ **VR:** Use VR journaling tools to reflect on the resilience dance experiences.

Day 3: Dance and Identity

Objective: Students will explore how dance can be used to express and explore personal and cultural identity.

Activities:

1. Identity Exploration:

○ **Traditional:** Reflect on personal and cultural identity and how it can be expressed through dance.

○ **VR:** Use VR journaling tools to document personal and cultural identity stories.

2. Creating an Identity Dance:

○ **Traditional:** Create a dance piece that represents personal or cultural identity.

○ **VR:** Use VR dance tools to design and share an identity dance routine.

3. Case Study:

○ **Traditional:** Study the case of Akram Khan, focusing on how he blends contemporary and traditional dance to explore identity.

○ **VR:** Use VR to explore virtual performances by Akram Khan and discuss his exploration of identity.

4. Reflection:

○ **Traditional:** Reflect on the identity dance activities and their impact on understanding and expressing identity through movement.

○ **VR:** Use VR journaling tools to reflect on the identity dance experiences.

Day 4: Dance and Collaboration

Objective: Students will understand the importance of collaboration in dance and how it fosters empathy and teamwork.

Activities:

1. Collaborative Dance Creation:

   ○ **Traditional:** Work in groups to create a dance piece that requires collaboration and teamwork.

   ○ **VR:** Collaborate on virtual dance projects using VR platforms.

2. Group Performance:

○ **Traditional:** Perform the collaborative dance piece and discuss the process of working together.

   ○ **VR:** Use VR to create and share a virtual group dance performance.

3. Case Study:

○ **Traditional:** Study the case of Pilobolus Dance Theater, focusing on their collaborative approach to dance creation.

   ○ **VR:** Use VR to explore virtual performances by Pilobolus and discuss their collaborative methods.

4. Reflection:

○ **Traditional:** Reflect on the collaborative dance activities and their impact on understanding teamwork and empathy through dance.

   ○ **VR:** Use VR journaling tools to reflect on the collaborative dance experiences.

Day 5: Dance and Healing

Objective: Students will explore how dance can be used as a tool for healing and emotional well-being.

Activities:

1. Healing through Movement:

o **Traditional:** Discuss how dance can be used for emotional healing and well-being.

o **VR:** Use VR dance experiences to explore how movement can foster healing.

2. Creating a Healing Dance:

o **Traditional:** Create a dance piece that focuses on healing and emotional well-being.

o **VR:** Use VR dance tools to design and share a healing dance routine.

3. Case Study:

o **Traditional:** Study the case of Dance Movement Therapy, focusing on how it is used for emotional healing.

o **VR:** Use VR to explore virtual Dance Movement Therapy sessions and discuss their impact.

4. Reflection:

o **Traditional:** Reflect on the healing dance activities and their impact on understanding and fostering emotional well-being through movement.

o **VR:** Use VR journaling tools to reflect on the healing dance experiences.

Week 16 Lesson Plans

Day 1: Creative Writing and Empathy

Objective: Students will use creative writing to explore and express empathy.

Activities:

1. Empathy Prompts:

   o **Traditional:** Provide writing prompts that encourage students to write from the perspective of someone else.

   o **VR:** Use VR creative writing tools to visualize and write stories from different perspectives.

2. Peer Review:

o **Traditional:** Students share their stories with peers and provide empathetic feedback.

   o **VR:** Use VR platforms to share and review stories in a virtual writing workshop.

3. Case Study:

o **Traditional:** Study the case of "The Diary of Anne Frank," focusing on how writing can convey deep empathy and understanding.

   o **VR:** Use VR to explore a virtual exhibit of Anne Frank's house and discuss the impact of her diary.

4. Reflection:

o **Traditional:** Reflect on how writing from another perspective can enhance empathy.

   o **VR:** Use VR journaling tools to reflect on the creative writing experience.

Day 2: Storytelling and Emotional Intelligence

Objective: Students will use storytelling to develop emotional intelligence and self-awareness.

Activities:

1. Personal Storytelling:

○ **Traditional:** Share personal stories that highlight emotional experiences and growth.

○ **VR:** Use VR storytelling tools to create and share personal narratives.

2. Character Analysis:

○ **Traditional:** Analyze characters in literature and their emotional journeys.

○ **VR:** Create VR scenarios where students can interact with characters and explore their perspectives.

3. Case Study:

○ **Traditional:** Study the case of "To Kill a Mockingbird" by Harper Lee, focusing on how storytelling can develop emotional intelligence.

○ **VR:** Use VR to explore scenes from "To Kill a Mockingbird" and discuss their impact.

4. Reflection:

○ **Traditional:** Reflect on the storytelling activities and their impact on emotional intelligence.

○ **VR:** Use VR journaling tools to reflect on the storytelling experiences.

Day 3: Poetry and Self-Expression

Objective: Students will use poetry to express their emotions and experiences.

Activities:

1. Poetry Writing:

- **Traditional:** Write poems that express personal emotions and experiences.
- **VR:** Use VR poetry creation tools to design and share poetic works.

2. Poetry Reading:

- **Traditional:** Share and read poems aloud, focusing on the emotional impact of the words.
- **VR:** Use VR platforms to host virtual poetry readings.

3. Case Study:

- **Traditional:** Study the case of Maya Angelou's poetry, focusing on how she uses poetry to express her life experiences and emotions.
- **VR:** Use VR to explore virtual readings of Maya Angelou's poetry and discuss their impact.

4. Reflection:

- **Traditional:** Reflect on the poetry writing and reading activities and their impact on self-expression.
- **VR:** Use VR journaling tools to reflect on the poetry experiences.

Day 4: Storytelling and Cultural Understanding

Objective: Students will use storytelling to explore and understand different cultures.

Activities:

1. Cultural Storytelling:

○ **Traditional:** Research and share stories from different cultures.

○ **VR:** Use VR to explore and share cultural stories from around the world.

2. Cultural Story Creation:

○ **Traditional:** Create stories that highlight cultural traditions and values.

○ **VR:** Use VR storytelling tools to design and share cultural narratives.

3. Case Study:

○ **Traditional:** Study the case of folktales from various cultures, focusing on how they convey cultural values and lessons.

○ **VR:** Use VR to explore virtual performances of cultural folktales and discuss their impact.

4. Reflection:

○ **Traditional:** Reflect on the cultural storytelling activities and their impact on understanding and appreciating different cultures.

○ **VR:** Use VR journaling tools to reflect on the cultural storytelling experiences.

Day 5: Storytelling and Community Building

Objective: Students will use storytelling to build a sense of community and foster inclusion.

Activities:

1. Community Storytelling:

○ **Traditional:** Share stories that highlight community experiences and values.

○ **VR:** Use VR to create and share virtual community stories.

2. Group Story Creation:

○ **Traditional:** Work in groups to create a story that represents the class or school community.

○ **VR:** Collaborate on virtual storytelling projects using VR platforms.

3. Case Study:

○ **Traditional:** Study the case of "Humans of New York," focusing on how storytelling can build community and foster inclusion.

○ **VR:** Use VR to explore virtual exhibits of "Humans of New York" and discuss their impact.

4. Reflection:

○ **Traditional:** Reflect on the community storytelling activities and their impact on building a sense of belonging and inclusion.

○ **VR:** Use VR journaling tools to reflect on the community storytelling experiences.

Week 17 Lesson Plans

Day 1: Visual Arts and Storytelling

Objective: Students will explore how visual arts can be used to tell stories and convey emotions.

Activities:

1. Visual Story Creation:
  ○ **Traditional:** Create a series of drawings or paintings that tell a story.
  ○ **VR:** Use VR art tools to design and share visual stories.

2. Art Gallery Walk:

  ○ **Traditional:** Organize a gallery walk where students display their visual stories and discuss their narratives.
  ○ **VR:** Use VR platforms to create a virtual art gallery and share visual stories.

3. Case Study:

○

Traditional:[1]Study[2]the[3]case[4]of[5]Frida[6]Kahlo,[7]focusing[8]on[9]how[10]she[1][1]used[12] her art to tell personal and emotional stories[13][14].

   ○ **VR:** Use VR to explore virtual exhibits of Frida Kahlo's work and discuss their storytelling elements.

4. Reflection:

○ **Traditional:** Reflect on the visual storytelling activities and their impact on understanding and expressing emotions through art.

   ○ **VR:** Use VR journaling tools to reflect on the visual storytelling experiences.

Day 2: Music and Emotional Expression

Objective: Students will explore how music can be used to express emotions and tell stories.

---

1. https://atelierkristel.com/art-of-storytelling-narratives-in-visual-art/

2. https://atelierkristel.com/art-of-storytelling-narratives-in-visual-art/

3. https://atelierkristel.com/art-of-storytelling-narratives-in-visual-art/

4. https://atelierkristel.com/art-of-storytelling-narratives-in-visual-art/

5. https://atelierkristel.com/art-of-storytelling-narratives-in-visual-art/

6. https://atelierkristel.com/art-of-storytelling-narratives-in-visual-art/

7. https://atelierkristel.com/art-of-storytelling-narratives-in-visual-art/

8. https://atelierkristel.com/art-of-storytelling-narratives-in-visual-art/

9. https://atelierkristel.com/art-of-storytelling-narratives-in-visual-art/

10. https://atelierkristel.com/art-of-storytelling-narratives-in-visual-art/

11. https://atelierkristel.com/art-of-storytelling-narratives-in-visual-art/

12. https://atelierkristel.com/art-of-storytelling-narratives-in-visual-art/

13. https://atelierkristel.com/art-of-storytelling-narratives-in-visual-art/

14. https://atelierkristel.com/art-of-storytelling-narratives-in-visual-art/

Activities:

1. Music Composition:

○ **Traditional:** Compose a piece of music that tells a story or conveys a specific emotion.

○ **VR:** Use VR music creation tools to design and share musical stories.

2. Music Listening and Analysis:

○ **Traditional:** Listen to and analyze pieces of music that tell stories or convey emotions.

○ **VR:** Use VR platforms to explore and analyze musical compositions.

3. Case Study:

○ **Traditional:** Study the case of Ludwig van Beethoven's "Symphony No. 9,"[15] focusing[16] on[17] how[18] it[19] conveys[20] a[21] powerful[22] narrative[23] and[2] [4]emotional[25] journey[26][27].

---

15. https://atelierkristel.com/art-of-storytelling-narratives-in-visual-art/

16. https://atelierkristel.com/art-of-storytelling-narratives-in-visual-art/

17. https://atelierkristel.com/art-of-storytelling-narratives-in-visual-art/

18. https://atelierkristel.com/art-of-storytelling-narratives-in-visual-art/

19. https://atelierkristel.com/art-of-storytelling-narratives-in-visual-art/

20. https://atelierkristel.com/art-of-storytelling-narratives-in-visual-art/

21. https://atelierkristel.com/art-of-storytelling-narratives-in-visual-art/

22. https://atelierkristel.com/art-of-storytelling-narratives-in-visual-art/

23. https://atelierkristel.com/art-of-storytelling-narratives-in-visual-art/

24. https://atelierkristel.com/art-of-storytelling-narratives-in-visual-art/

25. https://atelierkristel.com/art-of-storytelling-narratives-in-visual-art/

26. https://atelierkristel.com/art-of-storytelling-narratives-in-visual-art/

27. https://ingostudio.com/storytelling/visual-storytelling/

○ **VR:** Use VR to explore virtual performances of Beethoven's "Symphony No. 9" and discuss its storytelling elements.

4. Reflection:

○ **Traditional:** Reflect on the music composition and analysis activities and their impact on understanding and expressing emotions through music.

○ **VR:** Use VR journaling tools to reflect on the musical storytelling experiences.

Day 3: Visual Arts and Cultural Stories

Objective: Students will explore how visual arts can be used to tell cultural stories and foster empathy.

Activities:

1. Cultural Art Exploration:

○ **Traditional:** Research and create art pieces that represent cultural stories and traditions.

○ **VR:** Use VR art tools to design and share cultural visual stories.

2. Cultural Art Presentation:

○ **Traditional:** Present and discuss the cultural art pieces and their narratives.

○ **VR:** Use VR platforms to create a virtual exhibit of cultural art stories.

3. Case Study:

○

Traditional:[28]Study[29]the[30]case[31]of[32]traditional[33]Aboriginal[34]art,[3][5]focusing[36]on[37] how[38]it[39]conveys[40]cultural[41]stories[42]and[43]heritage[44][45].

○ **VR:** Use VR to explore virtual exhibits of Aboriginal art and discuss their storytelling elements.

4. Reflection:

○ **Traditional:** Reflect on the cultural art activities and their impact on understanding and appreciating different cultures through visual storytelling.

○ **VR:** Use VR journaling tools to reflect on the cultural art experiences.

28. https://atelierkristel.com/art-of-storytelling-narratives-in-visual-art/

29. https://atelierkristel.com/art-of-storytelling-narratives-in-visual-art/

30. https://atelierkristel.com/art-of-storytelling-narratives-in-visual-art/

31. https://atelierkristel.com/art-of-storytelling-narratives-in-visual-art/

32. https://atelierkristel.com/art-of-storytelling-narratives-in-visual-art/

33. https://atelierkristel.com/art-of-storytelling-narratives-in-visual-art/

34. https://atelierkristel.com/art-of-storytelling-narratives-in-visual-art/

35. https://atelierkristel.com/art-of-storytelling-narratives-in-visual-art/

36. https://atelierkristel.com/art-of-storytelling-narratives-in-visual-art/

37. https://atelierkristel.com/art-of-storytelling-narratives-in-visual-art/

38. https://atelierkristel.com/art-of-storytelling-narratives-in-visual-art/

39. https://atelierkristel.com/art-of-storytelling-narratives-in-visual-art/

40. https://atelierkristel.com/art-of-storytelling-narratives-in-visual-art/

41. https://atelierkristel.com/art-of-storytelling-narratives-in-visual-art/

42. https://atelierkristel.com/art-of-storytelling-narratives-in-visual-art/

43. https://atelierkristel.com/art-of-storytelling-narratives-in-visual-art/

44. https://atelierkristel.com/art-of-storytelling-narratives-in-visual-art/

45. https://brilliantio.com/visual-storytelling/

Day 4: Music and Personal Stories

Objective: Students will use music to express their own personal stories and experiences.

Activities:

1. Personal Music Composition:

　○ **Traditional:** Compose a piece of music that tells a personal story or experience.

　○ **VR:** Use VR music creation tools to design and share personal musical stories.

2. Music Sharing Session:

○ **Traditional:** Share and discuss the personal music compositions and their narratives.

　○ **VR:** Use VR platforms to host a virtual music sharing session.

3. Case Study:

○

Traditional: [46]Study[47]the[48]case[49]of[50]Billie[51]Eilish,[52]focusing[53]on[54]how[5]

---

46. https://atelierkristel.com/art-of-storytelling-narratives-in-visual-art/

47. https://atelierkristel.com/art-of-storytelling-narratives-in-visual-art/

48. https://atelierkristel.com/art-of-storytelling-narratives-in-visual-art/

49. https://atelierkristel.com/art-of-storytelling-narratives-in-visual-art/

50. https://atelierkristel.com/art-of-storytelling-narratives-in-visual-art/

51. https://atelierkristel.com/art-of-storytelling-narratives-in-visual-art/

52. https://atelierkristel.com/art-of-storytelling-narratives-in-visual-art/

53. https://atelierkristel.com/art-of-storytelling-narratives-in-visual-art/

54. https://atelierkristel.com/art-of-storytelling-narratives-in-visual-art/

55. https://atelierkristel.com/art-of-storytelling-narratives-in-visual-art/

[5]she[56]uses[57] her music to express personal experiences and emotions[58][459].

○ **VR:** Use VR to explore virtual performances of Billie Eilish's music and discuss their storytelling elements.

4. Reflection:

○ **Traditional:** Reflect on the personal music composition activities and their impact on self-expression and emotional release.

○ **VR:** Use VR journaling tools to reflect on the personal music experiences.

Day 5: Visual Arts, Music, and Community Building

Objective: Students will use visual arts and music to build a sense of community and foster inclusion.

Activities:

1. Community Art and Music Project:

○ **Traditional:** Work in groups to create a combined visual art and music project that represents the class or school community.

○ **VR:** Collaborate on virtual art and music projects using VR platforms.

2. Group Presentation:

○ **Traditional:** Present the community art and music projects and discuss their narratives.

○ **VR:** Use VR platforms to create a virtual exhibit of community art and music stories.

---

56. https://atelierkristel.com/art-of-storytelling-narratives-in-visual-art/

57. https://atelierkristel.com/art-of-storytelling-narratives-in-visual-art/

58. https://atelierkristel.com/art-of-storytelling-narratives-in-visual-art/

59. https://fromlight2art.com/music-and-visual-art/

3. Case Study:

○ **Traditional:** Study the case of the "Playing For Change" project, focusing on how it uses music to connect and build communities around the world.

    ○ **VR:** Use VR to explore virtual performances by "Playing For Change" and discuss their impact.

4. Reflection:

○ **Traditional:** Reflect on the community art and music activities and their impact on building a sense of belonging and inclusion.

    ○ **VR:** Use VR journaling tools to reflect on the community art and music experiences.

Week 18 Lesson Plans

Day 1: Introduction to Music Genres

Objective: Students will explore different music genres and understand their unique characteristics.

Activities:

1. Genre Exploration:

○ **Traditional:** Listen to and discuss examples of different music genres (e.g., classical, jazz, rock, hip-hop, electronic).

○ **VR:** Use VR music platforms to explore and experience different music genres.

2. Genre Characteristics:

○ **Traditional:** Create a chart that outlines the key characteristics of each genre.

○ **VR:** Use VR tools to create interactive charts and presentations on music genres.

3. Case Study:

○ **Traditional:**[1]Study[2]the[3]case[4]of[5]how[6]jazz[7]evolved[8]from[9]blues[10]and[11] ragtime, focusing on its cultural and historical significance[12][13].

---

1. https://www.twinkl.com/resources/art-and-design-extra-subjects-parents/music-extra-subjects-parents/musical-genres-music-extra-subjects-parents

2. https://www.twinkl.com/resources/art-and-design-extra-subjects-parents/music-extra-subjects-parents/musical-genres-music-extra-subjects-parents

3. https://www.twinkl.com/resources/art-and-design-extra-subjects-parents/music-extra-subjects-parents/musical-genres-music-extra-subjects-parents

4. https://www.twinkl.com/resources/art-and-design-extra-subjects-parents/music-extra-subjects-parents/musical-genres-music-extra-subjects-parents

○ **VR:** Use VR to explore virtual jazz performances and discuss their impact.

4. Reflection:

○ **Traditional:** Reflect on the genre exploration activities and their impact on understanding different music styles.

○ **VR:** Use VR journaling tools to reflect on the genre exploration experiences.

Day 2: Classical Music Composition

Objective: Students will compose a piece of music in the classical genre.

---

5. https://www.twinkl.com/resources/art-and-design-extra-subjects-parents/music-extra-subjects-parents/musical-genres-music-extra-subjects-parents

6. https://www.twinkl.com/resources/art-and-design-extra-subjects-parents/music-extra-subjects-parents/musical-genres-music-extra-subjects-parents

7. https://www.twinkl.com/resources/art-and-design-extra-subjects-parents/music-extra-subjects-parents/musical-genres-music-extra-subjects-parents

8. https://www.twinkl.com/resources/art-and-design-extra-subjects-parents/music-extra-subjects-parents/musical-genres-music-extra-subjects-parents

9. https://www.twinkl.com/resources/art-and-design-extra-subjects-parents/music-extra-subjects-parents/musical-genres-music-extra-subjects-parents

10. https://www.twinkl.com/resources/art-and-design-extra-subjects-parents/music-extra-subjects-parents/musical-genres-music-extra-subjects-parents

11. https://www.twinkl.com/resources/art-and-design-extra-subjects-parents/music-extra-subjects-parents/musical-genres-music-extra-subjects-parents

12. https://www.twinkl.com/resources/art-and-design-extra-subjects-parents/music-extra-subjects-parents/musical-genres-music-extra-subjects-parents

13. https://www.twinkl.com/resources/art-and-design-extra-subjects-parents/music-extra-subjects-parents/musical-genres-music-extra-subjects-parents

Activities:

1. Classical Composition Techniques:

○ **Traditional:** Teach basic classical composition techniques, such as counterpoint and harmony.

○ **VR:** Use VR music composition tools to practice classical techniques.

2. Classical Piece Creation:

○ **Traditional:** Compose a short piece of music in the classical style.

○ **VR:** Use VR music creation tools to design and share classical compositions.

3. Case Study:

○

Traditional: [14]Study[15]the[16]case[17]of[18]Wolfgang[19]Amadeus[20]Mozart,[2][1]focusing[22] on his contributions to classical music[23][24].

○ **VR:** Use VR to explore virtual performances of Mozart's works and discuss their impact.

4. Reflection:

○ **Traditional:** Reflect on the classical composition activities and their impact on understanding classical music.

---

14. https://www.twinkl.com/resources/art-and-design-extra-subjects-parents/music-extra-subjects-parents/musical-genres-music-extra-subjects-parents

15. https://www.twinkl.com/resources/art-and-design-extra-subjects-parents/music-extra-subjects-parents/musical-genres-music-extra-subjects-parents

16. https://www.twinkl.com/resources/art-and-design-extra-subjects-parents/music-extra-subjects-parents/musical-genres-music-extra-subjects-parents

17. https://www.twinkl.com/resources/art-and-design-extra-subjects-parents/music-extra-subjects-parents/musical-genres-music-extra-subjects-parents

18. https://www.twinkl.com/resources/art-and-design-extra-subjects-parents/music-extra-subjects-parents/musical-genres-music-extra-subjects-parents

19. https://www.twinkl.com/resources/art-and-design-extra-subjects-parents/music-extra-subjects-parents/musical-genres-music-extra-subjects-parents

20. https://www.twinkl.com/resources/art-and-design-extra-subjects-parents/music-extra-subjects-parents/musical-genres-music-extra-subjects-parents

21. https://www.twinkl.com/resources/art-and-design-extra-subjects-parents/music-extra-subjects-parents/musical-genres-music-extra-subjects-parents

22. https://www.twinkl.com/resources/art-and-design-extra-subjects-parents/music-extra-subjects-parents/musical-genres-music-extra-subjects-parents

23. https://www.twinkl.com/resources/art-and-design-extra-subjects-parents/music-extra-subjects-parents/musical-genres-music-extra-subjects-parents

24. https://www.composeyourmusic.com/course/music-composition-devices/

○ **VR:** Use VR journaling tools to reflect on the classical composition experiences.

Day 3: Jazz Music Composition

Objective: Students will compose a piece of music in the jazz genre.

Activities:

1. Jazz Composition Techniques:

○ **Traditional:** Teach basic jazz composition techniques, such as improvisation and swing rhythm.

○ **VR:** Use VR music composition tools to practice jazz techniques.

2. Jazz Piece Creation:

○ **Traditional:** Compose a short piece of music in the jazz style.

○ **VR:** Use VR music creation tools to design and share jazz compositions.

3. Case Study:

○

Traditional:[25]Study[26]the[27]case[28]of[29]Duke[30]Ellington,[31]focusing[32]on[3][3]his[34] contributions to jazz music[35][36].

   ○ **VR:** Use VR to explore virtual performances of Duke Ellington's works and discuss their impact.

---

25. https://www.twinkl.com/resources/art-and-design-extra-subjects-parents/music-extra-subjects-parents/musical-genres-music-extra-subjects-parents

26. https://www.twinkl.com/resources/art-and-design-extra-subjects-parents/music-extra-subjects-parents/musical-genres-music-extra-subjects-parents

27. https://www.twinkl.com/resources/art-and-design-extra-subjects-parents/music-extra-subjects-parents/musical-genres-music-extra-subjects-parents

28. https://www.twinkl.com/resources/art-and-design-extra-subjects-parents/music-extra-subjects-parents/musical-genres-music-extra-subjects-parents

29. https://www.twinkl.com/resources/art-and-design-extra-subjects-parents/music-extra-subjects-parents/musical-genres-music-extra-subjects-parents

30. https://www.twinkl.com/resources/art-and-design-extra-subjects-parents/music-extra-subjects-parents/musical-genres-music-extra-subjects-parents

31. https://www.twinkl.com/resources/art-and-design-extra-subjects-parents/music-extra-subjects-parents/musical-genres-music-extra-subjects-parents

32. https://www.twinkl.com/resources/art-and-design-extra-subjects-parents/music-extra-subjects-parents/musical-genres-music-extra-subjects-parents

33. https://www.twinkl.com/resources/art-and-design-extra-subjects-parents/music-extra-subjects-parents/musical-genres-music-extra-subjects-parents

34. https://www.twinkl.com/resources/art-and-design-extra-subjects-parents/music-extra-subjects-parents/musical-genres-music-extra-subjects-parents

35. https://www.twinkl.com/resources/art-and-design-extra-subjects-parents/music-extra-subjects-parents/musical-genres-music-extra-subjects-parents

36. https://themusiccrew.com/ideas-and-resources-for-teaching-composition/

4. Reflection:

○ **Traditional:** Reflect on the jazz composition activities and their impact on understanding jazz music.

  ○ **VR:** Use VR journaling tools to reflect on the jazz composition experiences.

Day 4: Rock Music Composition

Objective: Students will compose a piece of music in the rock genre.

Activities:

1. Rock Composition Techniques:

  ○ **Traditional:** Teach basic rock composition techniques, such as power chords and song structure.

  ○ **VR:** Use VR music composition tools to practice rock techniques.

2. Rock Piece Creation:

○ **Traditional:** Compose a short piece of music in the rock style.

  ○ **VR:** Use VR music creation tools to design and share rock compositions.

3. Case Study:

○

Traditional:[37] Study[38] the[39] case[40] of[41] The[42] Beatles,[43] focusing[44] on[45] their[46] contributions to rock music[47,48].

37. https://www.twinkl.com/resources/art-and-design-extra-subjects-parents/music-extra-subjects-parents/musical-genres-music-extra-subjects-parents

38. https://www.twinkl.com/resources/art-and-design-extra-subjects-parents/music-extra-subjects-parents/musical-genres-music-extra-subjects-parents

39. https://www.twinkl.com/resources/art-and-design-extra-subjects-parents/music-extra-subjects-parents/musical-genres-music-extra-subjects-parents

○ **VR:** Use VR to explore virtual performances of The Beatles' works and discuss their impact.

4. Reflection:

○ **Traditional:** Reflect on the rock composition activities and their impact on understanding rock music.

○ **VR:** Use VR journaling tools to reflect on the rock composition experiences.

Day 5: Hip-Hop Music Composition

Objective: Students will compose a piece of music in the hip-hop genre.

Activities:

1. Hip-Hop Composition Techniques:

40. https://www.twinkl.com/resources/art-and-design-extra-subjects-parents/music-extra-subjects-parents/musical-genres-music-extra-subjects-parents

41. https://www.twinkl.com/resources/art-and-design-extra-subjects-parents/music-extra-subjects-parents/musical-genres-music-extra-subjects-parents

42. https://www.twinkl.com/resources/art-and-design-extra-subjects-parents/music-extra-subjects-parents/musical-genres-music-extra-subjects-parents

43. https://www.twinkl.com/resources/art-and-design-extra-subjects-parents/music-extra-subjects-parents/musical-genres-music-extra-subjects-parents

44. https://www.twinkl.com/resources/art-and-design-extra-subjects-parents/music-extra-subjects-parents/musical-genres-music-extra-subjects-parents

45. https://www.twinkl.com/resources/art-and-design-extra-subjects-parents/music-extra-subjects-parents/musical-genres-music-extra-subjects-parents

46. https://www.twinkl.com/resources/art-and-design-extra-subjects-parents/music-extra-subjects-parents/musical-genres-music-extra-subjects-parents

47. https://www.twinkl.com/resources/art-and-design-extra-subjects-parents/music-extra-subjects-parents/musical-genres-music-extra-subjects-parents

48. https://online.berklee.edu/takenote/music-composition-techniques-and-resources/

○ **Traditional:** Teach basic hip-hop composition techniques, such as beat-making and lyric writing.

○ **VR:** Use VR music composition tools to practice hip-hop techniques.

2. Hip-Hop Piece Creation:

○ **Traditional:** Compose a short piece of music in the hip-hop style.

○ **VR:** Use VR music creation tools to design and share hip-hop compositions.

3. Case Study:

○

Traditional: [49]Study[50]the[51]case[52]of[53]Tupac[54]Shakur,[55]focusing[56]on[57]his[58] contributions to hip-hop music[59][60].

49. https://www.twinkl.com/resources/art-and-design-extra-subjects-parents/music-extra-subjects-parents/musical-genres-music-extra-subjects-parents

50. https://www.twinkl.com/resources/art-and-design-extra-subjects-parents/music-extra-subjects-parents/musical-genres-music-extra-subjects-parents

51. https://www.twinkl.com/resources/art-and-design-extra-subjects-parents/music-extra-subjects-parents/musical-genres-music-extra-subjects-parents

52. https://www.twinkl.com/resources/art-and-design-extra-subjects-parents/music-extra-subjects-parents/musical-genres-music-extra-subjects-parents

53. https://www.twinkl.com/resources/art-and-design-extra-subjects-parents/music-extra-subjects-parents/musical-genres-music-extra-subjects-parents

54. https://www.twinkl.com/resources/art-and-design-extra-subjects-parents/music-extra-subjects-parents/musical-genres-music-extra-subjects-parents

55. https://www.twinkl.com/resources/art-and-design-extra-subjects-parents/music-extra-subjects-parents/musical-genres-music-extra-subjects-parents

56. https://Twww.twinkl.com/Tesources/art-and-design-extra-subjects-parents/music-extra-subjects-parents/musical-genres-music-extra-subjects-parents

57. https://www.twinkl.com/resources/art-and-design-extra-subjects-parents/music-extra-subjects-parents/musical-genres-music-extra-subjects-parents

○ **VR:** Use VR to explore virtual performances of Tupac's works and discuss their impact.

4. Reflection:

○ **Traditional:** Reflect on the hip-hop composition activities and their impact on understanding hip-hop music.

○ **VR:** Use VR journaling tools to reflect on the hip-hop composition experiences.

58. https://www.twinkl.com/resources/art-and-design-extra-subjects-parents/music-extra-subjects-parents/musical-genres-music-extra-subjects-parents

59. https://www.twinkl.com/resources/art-and-design-extra-subjects-parents/music-extra-subjects-parents/musical-genres-music-extra-subjects-parents

60. https://www.beyondmusictheory.org/exercices-to-practice-your-music-composition-skills/

Week 19 Lesson Plans

Day 1: Introduction to Songwriting and Lyrics

Objective: Students will explore the basics of songwriting and lyric writing.

Activities:

1. Lyric Writing Prompts:
○ **Traditional:** Provide prompts that encourage students to write lyrics based on specific themes or emotions.

○ **VR:** Use VR writing tools to create and share lyrics inspired by virtual experiences.

2. Song Structure Analysis:

○ **Traditional:** Analyze the structure of popular songs to understand verse, chorus, and bridge.

○ **VR:** Use VR platforms to explore and deconstruct songs in a virtual music studio.

3. Case Study:

○

Traditional:[1]Study[2]the[3]case[4]of[5]Bob[6]Dylan,[7]focusing[8]on[9]his[10]lyric[11]writing[12] techniques and storytelling[13][14].

    ○ **VR:** Use VR to explore virtual performances of Bob Dylan's songs and discuss their lyrical impact.

4. Reflection:

○ **Traditional:** Reflect on the lyric writing and song structure activities and their impact on understanding songwriting.

    ○ **VR:** Use VR journaling tools to reflect on the songwriting experiences.

Day 2: Writing Lyrics from Personal Experience

Objective: Students will use personal experiences to write meaningful lyrics.

---

1. https://lyricworkroom.com/songwriting-prompts-and-lyric-writing-exercises/

2. https://lyricworkroom.com/songwriting-prompts-and-lyric-writing-exercises/

3. https://lyricworkroom.com/songwriting-prompts-and-lyric-writing-exercises/

4. https://lyricworkroom.com/songwriting-prompts-and-lyric-writing-exercises/

5. https://lyricworkroom.com/songwriting-prompts-and-lyric-writing-exercises/

6. https://lyricworkroom.com/songwriting-prompts-and-lyric-writing-exercises/

7. https://lyricworkroom.com/songwriting-prompts-and-lyric-writing-exercises/

8. https://lyricworkroom.com/songwriting-prompts-and-lyric-writing-exercises/

9. https://lyricworkroom.com/songwriting-prompts-and-lyric-writing-exercises/

10. https://lyricworkroom.com/songwriting-prompts-and-lyric-writing-exercises/

11. https://lyricworkroom.com/songwriting-prompts-and-lyric-writing-exercises/

12. https://lyricworkroom.com/songwriting-prompts-and-lyric-writing-exercises/

13. https://lyricworkroom.com/songwriting-prompts-and-lyric-writing-exercises/

14. https://lyricworkroom.com/songwriting-prompts-and-lyric-writing-exercises/

Activities:

1. Free Writing Exercise:

   o **Traditional:** Engage in a free writing exercise where students write about a personal experience.

   o **VR:** Use VR journaling tools to document personal stories and emotions.

2. Transforming Stories into Lyrics:

o **Traditional:** Transform the free writing exercise into song lyrics.

   o **VR:** Use VR lyric writing tools to create and share lyrics based on personal experiences.

3. Case Study:

o

Traditional: [15]Study[16]the[17]case[18]of[19]Taylor[20]Swift,[21]focusing[22]on[23]how[24]she[25]uses[26] personal experiences in her songwriting[27][28].

   o **VR:** Use VR to explore virtual performances of Taylor Swift's songs and discuss their lyrical storytelling.

---

15. https://lyricworkroom.com/songwriting-prompts-and-lyric-writing-exercises/

16. https://lyricworkroom.com/songwriting-prompts-and-lyric-writing-exercises/

17. https://lyricworkroom.com/songwriting-prompts-and-lyric-writing-exercises/

18. https://lyricworkroom.com/songwriting-prompts-and-lyric-writing-exercises/

19. https://lyricworkroom.com/songwriting-prompts-and-lyric-writing-exercises/

20. https://lyricworkroom.com/songwriting-prompts-and-lyric-writing-exercises/

21. https://lyricworkroom.com/songwriting-prompts-and-lyric-writing-exercises/

22. https://lyricworkroom.com/songwriting-prompts-and-lyric-writing-exercises/

23. https://lyricworkroom.com/songwriting-prompts-and-lyric-writing-exercises/

24. https://lyricworkroom.com/songwriting-prompts-and-lyric-writing-exercises/

25. https://lyricworkroom.com/songwriting-prompts-and-lyric-writing-exercises/

26. https://lyricworkroom.com/songwriting-prompts-and-lyric-writing-exercises/

27. https://lyricworkroom.com/songwriting-prompts-and-lyric-writing-exercises/

28. https://performerlife.com/best-songwriting-exercises/

4. Reflection:

○ **Traditional:** Reflect on the personal lyric writing activities and their impact on self-expression.

○ **VR:** Use VR journaling tools to reflect on the personal songwriting experiences.

Day 3: Collaborative Songwriting

Objective: Students will collaborate to write a song, fostering teamwork and creativity.

Activities:

1. Group Brainstorming:

○ **Traditional:** Work in groups to brainstorm song ideas and themes.

○ **VR:** Use VR collaboration tools to brainstorm and share ideas in a virtual music studio.

2. Collaborative Lyric Writing:

○ **Traditional:** Write song lyrics collaboratively, with each group member contributing.

○ **VR:** Use VR lyric writing tools to create and share collaborative lyrics.

3. Case Study:

○ **Traditional:** [29]Study the case of Lennon-McCartney, focusing on their[30] collaborative songwriting process[31][32].

---

29. https://lyricworkroom.com/songwriting-prompts-and-lyric-writing-exercises/

30. https://lyricworkroom.com/songwriting-prompts-and-lyric-writing-exercises/

31. https://lyricworkroom.com/songwriting-prompts-and-lyric-writing-exercises/

32. https://improvesongwriting.com/songwriting-exercises/

○ **VR:** Use VR to explore virtual performances of The Beatles' songs and discuss their collaborative techniques.

4. Reflection:

○ **Traditional:** Reflect on the collaborative songwriting activities and their impact on teamwork and creativity.

○ **VR:** Use VR journaling tools to reflect on the collaborative songwriting experiences.

Day 4: Writing Lyrics for Different Genres

Objective: Students will explore writing lyrics for different music genres.

Activities:

1. Genre Exploration:

○ **Traditional:** Listen to and discuss examples of lyrics from different music genres (e.g., pop, rock, country, hip-hop).

○ **VR:** Use VR music platforms to explore and analyze lyrics from various genres.

2. Genre-Specific Lyric Writing:

○ **Traditional:** Write song lyrics in a specific genre, focusing on its unique characteristics.

○ **VR:** Use VR lyric writing tools to create and share genre-specific lyrics.

3. Case Study:

o

Traditional:[33]Study[34]the[35]case[36]of[37]Kendrick[38]Lamar,[39]focusing[40]on[4] [1]his[42]lyric[43] writing in the hip-hop genre[44][45].

o **VR:** Use VR to explore virtual performances of Kendrick Lamar's songs and discuss their lyrical impact.

4. Reflection:

o **Traditional:** Reflect on the genre-specific lyric writing activities and their impact on understanding different music styles.

o **VR:** Use VR journaling tools to reflect on the genre-specific songwriting experiences.

Day 5: Performance and Feedback

Objective: Students will perform their songs and receive constructive feedback.

---

33. https://lyricworkroom.com/songwriting-prompts-and-lyric-writing-exercises/

34. https://lyricworkroom.com/songwriting-prompts-and-lyric-writing-exercises/

35. https://lyricworkroom.com/songwriting-prompts-and-lyric-writing-exercises/

36. https://lyricworkroom.com/songwriting-prompts-and-lyric-writing-exercises/

37. https://lyricworkroom.com/songwriting-prompts-and-lyric-writing-exercises/

38. https://lyricworkroom.com/songwriting-prompts-and-lyric-writing-exercises/

39. https://lyricworkroom.com/songwriting-prompts-and-lyric-writing-exercises/

40. https://lyricworkroom.com/songwriting-prompts-and-lyric-writing-exercises/

41. https://lyricworkroom.com/songwriting-prompts-and-lyric-writing-exercises/

42. https://lyricworkroom.com/songwriting-prompts-and-lyric-writing-exercises/

43. https://lyricworkroom.com/songwriting-prompts-and-lyric-writing-exercises/

44. https://lyricworkroom.com/songwriting-prompts-and-lyric-writing-exercises/

45. https://musicimpactnetwork.org/3-quick-songwriting-activities

Activities:

1. Song Performance:

○ **Traditional:** Perform the written songs in front of the class and discuss the lyrics.

○ **VR:** Use VR platforms to create and share virtual performances of the songs.

2. Peer Feedback:

○ **Traditional:** Provide constructive feedback on each other's performances and lyrics.

○ **VR:** Use VR collaboration tools to give and receive feedback in a virtual music studio.

3. Case Study:

○ **Traditional:**[46]Study[47]the[48]case[49]of[50]Adele,[51]focusing[52]on[53]her[54]live[55] performances[56]and[57]how[58]she[59]connects[60]with[61]her[62]audience[6] [3]through[64] lyrics[65][566].

   ○ **VR:** Use VR to explore virtual performances of Adele's songs and discuss their emotional impact.

4. Reflection:

○ **Traditional:** Reflect on the performance and feedback activities and their impact on songwriting and self-expression.

---

46. https://lyricworkroom.com/songwriting-prompts-and-lyric-writing-exercises/

47. https://lyricworkroom.com/songwriting-prompts-and-lyric-writing-exercises/

48. https://lyricworkroom.com/songwriting-prompts-and-lyric-writing-exercises/

49. https://lyricworkroom.com/songwriting-prompts-and-lyric-writing-exercises/

50. https://lyricworkroom.com/songwriting-prompts-and-lyric-writing-exercises/

51. https://lyricworkroom.com/songwriting-prompts-and-lyric-writing-exercises/

52. https://lyricworkroom.com/songwriting-prompts-and-lyric-writing-exercises/

53. https://lyricworkroom.com/songwriting-prompts-and-lyric-writing-exercises/

54. https://lyricworkroom.com/songwriting-prompts-and-lyric-writing-exercises/

55. https://lyricworkroom.com/songwriting-prompts-and-lyric-writing-exercises/

56. https://lyricworkroom.com/songwriting-prompts-and-lyric-writing-exercises/

57. https://lyricworkroom.com/songwriting-prompts-and-lyric-writing-exercises/

58. https://lyricworkroom.com/songwriting-prompts-and-lyric-writing-exercises/

59. https://lyricworkroom.com/songwriting-prompts-and-lyric-writing-exercises/

60. https://lyricworkroom.com/songwriting-prompts-and-lyric-writing-exercises/

61. https://lyricworkroom.com/songwriting-prompts-and-lyric-writing-exercises/

62. https://lyricworkroom.com/songwriting-prompts-and-lyric-writing-exercises/

63. https://lyricworkroom.com/songwriting-prompts-and-lyric-writing-exercises/

64. https://lyricworkroom.com/songwriting-prompts-and-lyric-writing-exercises/

65. https://lyricworkroom.com/songwriting-prompts-and-lyric-writing-exercises/

66. https://emastered.com/blog/songwriting-exercises

○ **VR:** Use VR journaling tools to reflect on the performance experiences.

Week 20 Lesson Plans

Day 1: Introduction to Songwriting for Social Change

Objective: Students will explore the concept of songwriting for social change and its impact on society.

Activities:

1. Listening Session:

- ○ **Traditional:** Listen to and discuss songs that have been influential in social movements (e.g., "Imagine" by John Lennon, "Blowin' in the Wind" by Bob Dylan).
- ○ **VR:** Use VR music platforms to explore and experience songs that have driven social change.

2. Impact Discussion:

- ○ **Traditional:** Discuss the impact of these songs on social movements and their messages.
- ○ **VR:** Use VR collaboration tools to facilitate a virtual discussion on the impact of these songs.

3. Case Study:

○

Traditional:[1]Study[2]the[3]case[4]of[5]"We[6]Shall[7]Overcome,"[8]focusing[9]on[10]its[11] role in the Civil Rights Movement[12][13].

○ **VR:** Use VR to explore virtual performances and historical contexts of "We Shall Overcome."

4. Reflection:

○ **Traditional:** Reflect on the listening session and discussion activities and their impact on understanding songwriting for social change.

○ **VR:** Use VR journaling tools to reflect on the experiences.

Day 2: Identifying Social Issues

Objective: Students will identify social issues they are passionate about and brainstorm song ideas.

Activities:

1. Issue Brainstorming:

---

1. **https://www.grammy.com/awards/best-song-for-social-change-award**

2. https://www.grammy.com/awards/best-song-for-social-change-award

3. https://www.grammy.com/awards/best-song-for-social-change-award

4. https://www.grammy.com/awards/best-song-for-social-change-award

5. https://www.grammy.com/awards/best-song-for-social-change-award

6. https://www.grammy.com/awards/best-song-for-social-change-award

7. https://www.grammy.com/awards/best-song-for-social-change-award

8. https://www.grammy.com/awards/best-song-for-social-change-award

9. https://www.grammy.com/awards/best-song-for-social-change-award

10. https://www.grammy.com/awards/best-song-for-social-change-award

11. https://www.grammy.com/awards/best-song-for-social-change-award

12. https://www.grammy.com/awards/best-song-for-social-change-award

13. https://www.grammy.com/awards/best-song-for-social-change-award

○ **Traditional:** Brainstorm and list social issues that students care about (e.g., climate change, gender equality, racial justice).

○ **VR:** Use VR collaboration tools to brainstorm and share ideas in a virtual space.

2. Research and Inspiration:

○ **Traditional:** Research the chosen social issues and find inspiration from existing songs and movements.

○ **VR:** Use VR to explore virtual exhibits and resources related to the chosen social issues.

3. Case Study:

○

Traditional:[14]Study[15]the[16]case[17]of[18]"Fight[19]the[20]Power"[21]by[22]Public[23]Enemy,[24] focusing on its message and impact[25][26].

○ **VR:** Use VR to explore virtual performances and discussions about "Fight the Power."

---

14. https://www.grammy.com/awards/best-song-for-social-change-award

15. https://www.grammy.com/awards/best-song-for-social-change-award

16. https://www.grammy.com/awards/best-song-for-social-change-award

17. https://www.grammy.com/awards/best-song-for-social-change-award

18. https://www.grammy.com/awards/best-song-for-social-change-award

19. https://www.grammy.com/awards/best-song-for-social-change-award

20. https://www.grammy.com/awards/best-song-for-social-change-award

21. https://www.grammy.com/awards/best-song-for-social-change-award

22. https://www.grammy.com/awards/best-song-for-social-change-award

23. https://www.grammy.com/awards/best-song-for-social-change-award

24. https://Trawdir.grammy.com/Brawards/best-song-for-social-change-award

25. https://www.grammy.com/awards/best-song-for-social-change-award

26. https://college.berklee.edu/news/berklee-announces-2024-songs-for-social-change-contest-winners

4. Reflection:

○ **Traditional:** Reflect on the issue brainstorming and research activities and their impact on understanding social issues.

○ **VR:** Use VR journaling tools to reflect on the experiences.

Day 3: Writing Lyrics for Social Change

Objective: Students will write lyrics that address the social issues they are passionate about.

Activities:

1. Lyric Writing Workshop:

○ **Traditional:** Conduct a workshop on writing impactful lyrics that address social issues.

○ **VR:** Use VR lyric writing tools to create and share lyrics focused on social change.

2. Peer Review:

○ **Traditional:** Share and review each other's lyrics, providing constructive feedback.

○ **VR:** Use VR collaboration tools to facilitate a virtual lyric review session.

3. Case Study:

○

Traditional:[27]Study[28]the[29]case[30]of[31]"Alright"[32]by[33]Kendrick[34]Lamar,[35]focusing[36]on[37] its lyrical content and social impact[38][39].

○ **VR:** Use VR to explore virtual performances and discussions about "Alright."

4. Reflection:

○ **Traditional:** Reflect on the lyric writing workshop and peer review activities and their impact on songwriting for social change.

○ **VR:** Use VR journaling tools to reflect on the experiences.

Day 4: Composing Music for Social Change

Objective: Students will compose music that complements their lyrics and enhances the message of social change.

Activities:

1. Music Composition Techniques:

---

27. https://www.grammy.com/awards/best-song-for-social-change-award

28. https://www.grammy.com/awards/best-song-for-social-change-award

29. https://www.grammy.com/awards/best-song-for-social-change-award

30. https://www.grammy.com/awards/best-song-for-social-change-award

31. https://www.grammy.com/awards/best-song-for-social-change-award

32. https://www.grammy.com/awards/best-song-for-social-change-award

33. https://www.grammy.com/awards/best-song-for-social-change-award

34. https://www.grammy.com/awards/best-song-for-social-change-award

35. https://www.grammy.com/awards/best-song-for-social-change-award

36. https://www.grammy.com/awards/best-song-for-social-change-award

37. https://www.grammy.com/awards/best-song-for-social-change-award

38. https://www.grammy.com/awards/best-song-for-social-change-award

39. https://www.berklee.edu/news/berklee-now/twelve-songs-became-anthems-cultural-change

○ **Traditional:** Teach basic music composition techniques that can enhance the message of social change.

○ **VR:** Use VR music composition tools to practice and create music for social change.

2. Song Creation:

○ **Traditional:** Compose music that complements the lyrics written in the previous session.

○ **VR:** Use VR music creation tools to design and share complete songs focused on social change.

3. Case Study:

○

Traditional:[40]Study[41]the[42]case[43]of[44]"This[45]Is[46]America"[47]by[48]Childish[49]Gambino,[50] focusing on its musical composition and social commentary[51][452].

○ **VR:** Use VR to explore virtual performances and discussions about "This Is America."

---

40. https://www.grammy.com/awards/best-song-for-social-change-award

41. https://www.grammy.com/awards/best-song-for-social-change-award

42. https://www.grammy.com/awards/best-song-for-social-change-award

43. https://www.grammy.com/awards/best-song-for-social-change-award

44. https://www.grammy.com/awards/best-song-for-social-change-award

45. https://www.grammy.com/awards/best-song-for-social-change-award

46. https://www.grammy.com/awards/best-song-for-social-change-award

47. https://www.grammy.com/awards/best-song-for-social-change-award

48. https://www.grammy.com/awards/best-song-for-social-change-award

49. https://Twww.grammy.com/Teawards/best-song-for-social-change-award

50. https://www.grammy.com/awards/best-song-for-social-change-award

51. https://www.grammy.com/awards/best-song-for-social-change-award

52. https://repeatreplay.com/songs-for-social-change/

4. Reflection:

○ **Traditional:** Reflect on the music composition activities and their impact on creating songs for social change.

    ○ **VR:** Use VR journaling tools to reflect on the experiences.

Day 5: Performance and Advocacy

Objective: Students will perform their songs and discuss how they can use music to advocate for social change.

Activities:

1. Song Performance:

    ○ **Traditional:** Perform the completed songs in front of the class and discuss their messages.

    ○ **VR:** Use VR platforms to create and share virtual performances of the songs.

2. Advocacy Discussion:

○ **Traditional:** Discuss how students can use their songs to advocate for social change in their communities.

    ○ **VR:** Use VR collaboration tools to facilitate a virtual discussion on music and advocacy.

3. Case Study:

○

Traditional:[53]Study[54]the[55]case[56]of[57]"A[58]Change[59]Is[60]Gonna[61]Come"[6

---

53. https://www.grammy.com/awards/best-song-for-social-change-award

54. https://www.grammy.com/awards/best-song-for-social-change-award

55. https://www.grammy.com/awards/best-song-for-social-change-award

56. https://www.grammy.com/awards/best-song-for-social-change-award

57. https://www.grammy.com/awards/best-song-for-social-change-award

58. https://www.grammy.com/awards/best-song-for-social-change-award

59. https://www.grammy.com/awards/best-song-for-social-change-award

[2]by[63]Sam[64]

Cooke,[65]focusing[66]on[67]its[68]role[69]in[70]advocating[71]for[72]social[73]change[74][57][7].

○ **VR:** Use VR to explore virtual performances and discussions about "A Change Is Gonna Come."

4. Reflection:

○ **Traditional:** Reflect on the performance and advocacy activities and their impact on using music for social change.

○ **VR:** Use VR journaling tools to reflect on the experiences.

60. https://www.grammy.com/awards/best-song-for-social-change-award

61. https://www.grammy.com/awards/best-song-for-social-change-award

62. https://www.grammy.com/awards/best-song-for-social-change-award

63. https://www.grammy.com/awards/best-song-for-social-change-award

64. https://www.grammy.com/awards/best-song-for-social-change-award

65. https://www.grammy.com/awards/best-song-for-social-change-award

66. https://www.grammy.com/awards/best-song-for-social-change-award

67. https://www.grammy.com/awards/best-song-for-social-change-award

68. https://www.grammy.com/awards/best-song-for-social-change-award

69. https://www.grammy.com/awards/best-song-for-social-change-award

70. https://www.grammy.com/awards/best-song-for-social-change-award

71. https://www.grammy.com/awards/best-song-for-social-change-award

72. https://www.grammy.com/awards/best-song-for-social-change-award

73. https://www.grammy.com/awards/best-song-for-social-change-award

74. https://www.grammy.com/awards/best-song-for-social-change-award

75. https://audioassemble.com/songs-for-social-issues/

Week 21 Lesson Plans

Day 1: Introduction to Music Videos and Visual Storytelling

Objective: Students will explore the basics of music videos and visual storytelling.

Activities:

1. **Music Video Analysis:**

   ○ **Traditional:** Watch and analyze music videos that are known for their strong visual storytelling (e.g., "Thriller" by Michael Jackson, "Formation" by Beyoncé).

   ○ **VR:** Use VR platforms to explore and experience music videos in an immersive environment.

2. **Visual Storytelling Techniques:**

○

Traditional:[1]Discuss[2]techniques[3]used[4]in[5]visual[6]storytelling,[7]such[8]as[9] framing,[10]composition,[11]and[12]symbolism[13][14].

1. https://blog.novecore.com/the-power-of-music-videos-analyzing-cinematic-techniques/

2. https://blog.novecore.com/the-power-of-music-videos-analyzing-cinematic-techniques/

3. https://blog.novecore.com/the-power-of-music-videos-analyzing-cinematic-techniques/

4. https://blog.novecore.com/the-power-of-music-videos-analyzing-cinematic-techniques/

5. https://blog.novecore.com/the-power-of-music-videos-analyzing-cinematic-techniques/

6. https://blog.novecore.com/the-power-of-music-videos-analyzing-cinematic-techniques/

7. https://blog.novecore.com/the-power-of-music-videos-analyzing-cinematic-techniques/

8. https://blog.novecore.com/the-power-of-music-videos-analyzing-cinematic-techniques/

9. https://blog.novecore.com/the-power-of-music-videos-analyzing-cinematic-techniques/

10. https://blog.novecore.com/the-power-of-music-videos-analyzing-cinematic-techniques/

11. https://blog.novecore.com/the-power-of-music-videos-analyzing-cinematic-techniques/

12. https://blog.novecore.com/the-power-of-music-videos-analyzing-cinematic-techniques/

○ **VR:** Use VR tools to create and experiment with visual storytelling techniques.

3. Case Study:

○

Traditional:[15]Study[16]the[17]case[18]of[19]"Lemonade"[20]by[21]Beyoncé,[2][2]focusing[23]on[24]its[25] narrative and visual elements[26][27].

○ **VR:** Use VR to explore virtual performances and discussions about "Lemonade."

4. Reflection:

○ **Traditional:** Reflect on the music video analysis and visual storytelling activities and their impact on understanding visual narratives.

○ **VR:** Use VR journaling tools to reflect on the experiences.

---

13. https://blog.novecore.com/the-power-of-music-videos-analyzing-cinematic-techniques/

14. https://blog.novecore.com/the-power-of-music-videos-analyzing-cinematic-techniques/

15. https://blog.novecore.com/the-power-of-music-videos-analyzing-cinematic-techniques/

16. https://blog.novecore.com/the-power-of-music-videos-analyzing-cinematic-techniques/

17. https://blog.novecore.com/the-power-of-music-videos-analyzing-cinematic-techniques/

18. https://blog.novecore.com/the-power-of-music-videos-analyzing-cinematic-techniques/

19. https://blog.novecore.com/the-power-of-music-videos-analyzing-cinematic-techniques/

20. https://blog.novecore.com/the-power-of-music-videos-analyzing-cinematic-techniques/

21. https://blog.novecore.com/the-power-of-music-videos-analyzing-cinematic-techniques/

22. https://blog.novecore.com/the-power-of-music-videos-analyzing-cinematic-techniques/

23. https://blog.novecore.com/the-power-of-music-videos-analyzing-cinematic-techniques/

24. https://blog.novecore.com/the-power-of-music-videos-analyzing-cinematic-techniques/

25. https://blog.novecore.com/the-power-of-music-videos-analyzing-cinematic-techniques/

26. https://blog.novecore.com/the-power-of-music-videos-analyzing-cinematic-techniques/

27. https://openr.co/unveiling-the-artistry-how-music-videos-captivate-their-target-audiences/

Day 2: Creating a Storyboard for a Music Video

Objective: Students will learn how to create a storyboard for a music video.

Activities:

1. Storyboard Basics:

○ **Traditional:** Teach the basics of storyboarding, including how to plan shots and sequences.

○ **VR:** Use VR tools to create interactive storyboards.

2. Storyboard Creation:

○ **Traditional:** Create a storyboard for a music video based on a chosen song.

○ **VR:** Use VR platforms to design and share storyboards in a virtual environment.

3. Case Study:

○

Traditional:[28]Study[29]the[30]case[31]of[32]"This[33]Is[34]America"[35]by[36]Childish[3][7]Gambino,[38] focusing on its storyboard and visual planning[39][140].

28. https://blog.novecore.com/the-power-of-music-videos-analyzing-cinematic-techniques/

29. https://blog.novecore.com/the-power-of-music-videos-analyzing-cinematic-techniques/

30. https://blog.novecore.com/the-power-of-music-videos-analyzing-cinematic-techniques/

31. https://blog.novecore.com/the-power-of-music-videos-analyzing-cinematic-techniques/

32. https://blog.novecore.com/the-power-of-music-videos-analyzing-cinematic-techniques/

33. https://blog.novecore.com/the-power-of-music-videos-analyzing-cinematic-techniques/

34. https://blog.novecore.com/the-power-of-music-videos-analyzing-cinematic-techniques/

35. https://blog.novecore.com/the-power-of-music-videos-analyzing-cinematic-techniques/

36. https://blog.novecore.com/the-power-of-music-videos-analyzing-cinematic-techniques/

37. https://blog.novecore.com/the-power-of-music-videos-analyzing-cinematic-techniques/

38. https://blog.novecore.com/the-power-of-music-videos-analyzing-cinematic-techniques/

○ **VR:** Use VR to explore virtual discussions about the making of "This Is America."

4. Reflection:

○ **Traditional:** Reflect on the storyboard creation activities and their impact on planning visual narratives.

○ **VR:** Use VR journaling tools to reflect on the storyboard experiences.

Day 3: Filming and Editing a Music Video

Objective: Students will film and edit a music video based on their storyboard.

Activities:

1. Filming Techniques:

○ **Traditional:** Teach basic filming techniques, including camera angles, lighting, and shot composition.

○ **VR:** Use VR tools to practice filming techniques in a virtual environment.

2. Editing Basics:

○ **Traditional:** Teach basic editing techniques, including cutting, transitions, and effects.

○ **VR:** Use VR editing tools to create and share edited music videos.

---

39. https://blog.novecore.com/the-power-of-music-videos-analyzing-cinematic-techniques/

40. https://blog.novecore.com/the-power-of-music-videos-analyzing-cinematic-techniques/

3. Case Study:

o

Traditional: [41]Study[42]the[43]case[44]of[45]"Bad[46]Romance"[47]by[48]Lady[49]Gaga, [50]focusing[51] on its filming and editing techniques[52][53].

o **VR:** Use VR to explore virtual discussions about the making of "Bad Romance."

4. Reflection:

o **Traditional:** Reflect on the filming and editing activities and their impact on creating visual narratives.

o **VR:** Use VR journaling tools to reflect on the filming and editing experiences.

Day 4: Visual Storytelling and Social Change

Objective: Students will explore how music videos can be used to advocate for social change.

---

41. https://blog.novecore.com/the-power-of-music-videos-analyzing-cinematic-techniques/

42. https://blog.novecore.com/the-power-of-music-videos-analyzing-cinematic-techniques/

43. https://blog.novecore.com/the-power-of-music-videos-analyzing-cinematic-techniques/

44. https://blog.novecore.com/the-power-of-music-videos-analyzing-cinematic-techniques/

45. https://blog.novecore.com/the-power-of-music-videos-analyzing-cinematic-techniques/

46. https://blog.novecore.com/the-power-of-music-videos-analyzing-cinematic-techniques/

47. https://blog.novecore.com/the-power-of-music-videos-analyzing-cinematic-techniques/

48. https://blog.novecore.com/the-power-of-music-videos-analyzing-cinematic-techniques/

49. https://blog.novecore.com/the-power-of-music-videos-analyzing-cinematic-techniques/

50. https://blog.novecore.com/the-power-of-music-videos-analyzing-cinematic-techniques/

51. https://blog.novecore.com/the-power-of-music-videos-analyzing-cinematic-techniques/

52. https://blog.novecore.com/the-power-of-music-videos-analyzing-cinematic-techniques/

53. https://blog.novecore.com/the-power-of-music-videos-analyzing-cinematic-techniques/

Activities:

1. Social Change Music Videos:

○ **Traditional:** Watch and discuss music videos that address social issues (e.g., "Where Is the Love?" by The Black Eyed Peas, "Same Love" by Macklemore & Ryan Lewis).

○ **VR:** Use VR platforms to explore and experience music videos focused on social change.

2. Creating a Social Change Music Video:

○ **Traditional:** Plan and create a music video that addresses a social issue.

○ **VR:** Use VR tools to design and share music videos focused on social change.

3. Case Study:

○

Traditional:[54]Study[55]the[56]case[57]of[58]"This[59]Is[60]Me"[61]from[62]The[6][3]Greatest[64] Showman, focusing on its message and visual storytelling[65][166].

54. https://blog.novecore.com/the-power-of-music-videos-analyzing-cinematic-techniques/

55. https://blog.novecore.com/the-power-of-music-videos-analyzing-cinematic-techniques/

56. https://blog.novecore.com/the-power-of-music-videos-analyzing-cinematic-techniques/

57. https://blog.novecore.com/the-power-of-music-videos-analyzing-cinematic-techniques/

58. https://blog.novecore.com/the-power-of-music-videos-analyzing-cinematic-techniques/

59. https://blog.novecore.com/the-power-of-music-videos-analyzing-cinematic-techniques/

60. https://blog.novecore.com/the-power-of-music-videos-analyzing-cinematic-techniques/

61. https://blog.novecore.com/the-power-of-music-videos-analyzing-cinematic-techniques/

62. https://blog.novecore.com/the-power-of-music-videos-analyzing-cinematic-techniques/

63. https://blog.novecore.com/the-power-of-music-videos-analyzing-cinematic-techniques/

64. https://blog.novecore.com/the-power-of-music-videos-analyzing-cinematic-techniques/

65. https://blog.novecore.com/the-power-of-music-videos-analyzing-cinematic-techniques/

66. https://blog.novecore.com/the-power-of-music-videos-analyzing-cinematic-techniques/

○ **VR:** Use VR to explore virtual performances and discussions about "This Is Me."

4. Reflection:

○ **Traditional:** Reflect on the social change music video activities and their impact on using visual storytelling for advocacy.

○ **VR:** Use VR journaling tools to reflect on the social change music video experiences.

Day 5: Music Video Showcase and Feedback

Objective: Students will showcase their music videos and receive constructive feedback.

Activities:

1. Music Video Showcase:

○ **Traditional:** Present the completed music videos to the class and discuss their narratives.

○ **VR:** Use VR platforms to create and share virtual showcases of the music videos.

2. Peer Feedback:

○ **Traditional:** Provide constructive feedback on each other's music videos and visual storytelling techniques.

○ **VR:** Use VR collaboration tools to facilitate a virtual feedback session.

3. Case Study:

o

Traditional:[67]Study[68]the[69]case[70]of[71]"Formation"[72]by[73]Beyoncé,[7][4]focusing[75]on[76]its[77] reception and impact[78][279].

o **VR:** Use VR to explore virtual discussions about the impact of "Formation."

4. Reflection:

o **Traditional:** Reflect on the music video showcase and feedback activities and their impact on visual storytelling.

o **VR:** Use VR journaling tools to reflect on the showcase experiences.

67. https://blog.novecore.com/the-power-of-music-videos-analyzing-cinematic-techniques/

68. https://blog.novecore.com/the-power-of-music-videos-analyzing-cinematic-techniques/

69. https://blog.novecore.com/the-power-of-music-videos-analyzing-cinematic-techniques/

70. https://blog.novecore.com/the-power-of-music-videos-analyzing-cinematic-techniques/

71. https://blog.novecore.com/the-power-of-music-videos-analyzing-cinematic-techniques/

72. https://blog.novecore.com/the-power-of-music-videos-analyzing-cinematic-techniques/

73. https://blog.novecore.com/the-power-of-music-videos-analyzing-cinematic-techniques/

74. https://blog.novecore.com/the-power-of-music-videos-analyzing-cinematic-techniques/

75. https://blog.novecore.com/the-power-of-music-videos-analyzing-cinematic-techniques/

76. https://blog.novecore.com/the-power-of-music-videos-analyzing-cinematic-techniques/

77. https://blog.novecore.com/the-power-of-music-videos-analyzing-cinematic-techniques/

78. https://blog.novecore.com/the-power-of-music-videos-analyzing-cinematic-techniques/

79. https://openr.co/unveiling-the-artistry-how-music-videos-captivate-their-target-audiences/

Week 22 Lesson Plans: Stage Presence

Objective: Students will understand the basics of stage presence and its importance in live performances.

Activities:

1. Stage Presence Exploration:

○ **Traditional:** Discuss what stage presence is and why it's important for performers.

○ **VR:** Use VR platforms to explore examples of strong stage presence in virtual performances.

2. Body Language and Movement:

○ **Traditional:** Practice body language and movement exercises to enhance stage presence.

○ **VR:** Use VR tools to practice and analyze body language and movement in a virtual environment.

3. Case Study:

o

Traditional: [1]Study[2]the[3]case[4]of[5]Freddie[6]Mercury,[7]focusing[8]on[9]his[1][0]stage[11] presence and performance techniques[12][13].

o **VR:** Use VR to explore virtual performances of Freddie Mercury and discuss his stage presence.

4. Reflection:

o **Traditional:** Reflect on the stage presence exploration activities and their impact on understanding live performances.

o **VR:** Use VR journaling tools to reflect on the stage presence experiences.

Day 2: Building Confidence on Stage

Objective: Students will learn techniques to build confidence and overcome stage fright.

---

1. https://ledgernote.com/columns/gigs-live-performance/stage-presence/

2. https://ledgernote.com/columns/gigs-live-performance/stage-presence/

3. https://ledgernote.com/columns/gigs-live-performance/stage-presence/

4. https://ledgernote.com/columns/gigs-live-performance/stage-presence/

5. https://ledgernote.com/columns/gigs-live-performance/stage-presence/

6. https://ledgernote.com/columns/gigs-live-performance/stage-presence/

7. https://ledgernote.com/columns/gigs-live-performance/stage-presence/

8. https://ledgernote.com/columns/gigs-live-performance/stage-presence/

9. https://ledgernote.com/columns/gigs-live-performance/stage-presence/

10. https://ledgernote.com/columns/gigs-live-performance/stage-presence/

11. https://ledgernote.com/columns/gigs-live-performance/stage-presence/

12. https://ledgernote.com/columns/gigs-live-performance/stage-presence/

13. https://ledgernote.com/columns/gigs-live-performance/stage-presence/

Activities:

1. Confidence-Building Exercises:

 o **Traditional:** Engage in exercises that build confidence, such as positive affirmations and visualization.

 o **VR:** Use VR tools to practice confidence-building techniques in a virtual performance setting.

2. Overcoming Stage Fright:

o **Traditional:** Discuss strategies to overcome stage fright and practice relaxation techniques.

 o **VR:** Use VR platforms to simulate live performance scenarios and practice overcoming stage fright.

3. Case Study:

o

Traditional: [14]Study [15]the [16]case [17]of [18]Adele, [19]focusing [20]on [21]how [22]she [23]manages [24]stage fright and builds confidence [25][26].

 o **VR:** Use VR to explore virtual performances of Adele and discuss her techniques for overcoming stage fright.

---

14. https://ledgernote.com/columns/gigs-live-performance/stage-presence/

15. https://ledgernote.com/columns/gigs-live-performance/stage-presence/

16. https://ledgernote.com/columns/gigs-live-performance/stage-presence/

17. https://ledgernote.com/columns/gigs-live-performance/stage-presence/

18. https://ledgernote.com/columns/gigs-live-performance/stage-presence/

19. https://ledgernote.com/columns/gigs-live-performance/stage-presence/

20. https://ledgernote.com/columns/gigs-live-performance/stage-presence/

21. https://ledgernote.com/columns/gigs-live-performance/stage-presence/

22. https://ledgernote.com/columns/gigs-live-performance/stage-presence/

23. https://ledgernote.com/columns/gigs-live-performance/stage-presence/

24. https://ledgernote.com/columns/gigs-live-performance/stage-presence/

25. https://ledgernote.com/columns/gigs-live-performance/stage-presence/

26. https://blog.novecore.com/crafting-a-memorable-stage-presence-tips-for-live-performers/

4. Reflection:

○ **Traditional:** Reflect on the confidence-building activities and their impact on stage presence.

○ **VR:** Use VR journaling tools to reflect on the confidence-building experiences.

Day 3: Engaging with the Audience

Objective: Students will learn techniques to engage and connect with the audience during live performances.

Activities:

1. Audience Engagement Techniques:

○ **Traditional:** Practice techniques for engaging with the audience, such as eye contact, gestures, and interaction.

○ **VR:** Use VR tools to practice audience engagement in a virtual performance setting.

2. Interactive Performance:

○ **Traditional:** Perform a short piece and practice engaging with the audience.

○ **VR:** Use VR platforms to create and share interactive performances.

3. Case Study:

○

Traditional:[27]Study[28]the[29]case[30]of[31]Bruce[32]Springsteen,[33]focusing[34]on[3]

---

27. https://ledgernote.com/columns/gigs-live-performance/stage-presence/

28. https://ledgernote.com/columns/gigs-live-performance/stage-presence/

29. https://ledgernote.com/columns/gigs-live-performance/stage-presence/

30. https://ledgernote.com/columns/gigs-live-performance/stage-presence/

31. https://ledgernote.com/columns/gigs-live-performance/stage-presence/

[5]his[36] ability to connect with the audience during live performances[37,2,38].

○ **VR:** Use VR to explore virtual performances of Bruce Springsteen and discuss his audience engagement techniques.

4. Reflection:

○ **Traditional:** Reflect on the audience engagement activities and their impact on live performances.

○ **VR:** Use VR journaling tools to reflect on the audience engagement experiences.

Day 4: Choreography and Movement

Objective: Students will explore the role of choreography and movement in enhancing stage presence.

Activities:

1. Choreography Basics:

○ **Traditional:** Teach basic choreography techniques and how to incorporate movement into performances.

○ **VR:** Use VR tools to practice and create choreography in a virtual environment.

---

32. https://ledgernote.com/columns/gigs-live-performance/stage-presence/

33. https://ledgernote.com/columns/gigs-live-performance/stage-presence/

34. https://ledgernote.com/columns/gigs-live-performance/stage-presence/

35. https://ledgernote.com/columns/gigs-live-performance/stage-presence/

36. https://ledgernote.com/columns/gigs-live-performance/stage-presence/

37. https://ledgernote.com/columns/gigs-live-performance/stage-presence/

38. https://vocalist.org.uk/stage-presence

2. Movement Practice:

○ **Traditional:** Practice choreographed movements and integrate them into a performance piece.

○ **VR:** Use VR platforms to create and share choreographed performances.

3. Case Study:

○ **Traditional:**[39]Study[40]the[41]case[42]of[43]Beyoncé,[44]focusing[45]on[46]her[47] choreography and stage presence[48][49].

○ **VR:** Use VR to explore virtual performances of Beyoncé and discuss her choreography techniques.

4. Reflection:

○ **Traditional:** Reflect on the choreography and movement activities and their impact on stage presence.

○ **VR:** Use VR journaling tools to reflect on the choreography experiences.

Day 5: Live Performance Showcase

Objective: Students will showcase their live performance skills and receive constructive feedback.

---

39. https://ledgernote.com/columns/gigs-live-performance/stage-presence/

40. https://ledgernote.com/columns/gigs-live-performance/stage-presence/

41. https://ledgernote.com/columns/gigs-live-performance/stage-presence/

42. https://ledgernote.com/columns/gigs-live-performance/stage-presence/

43. https://ledgernote.com/columns/gigs-live-performance/stage-presence/

44. https://ledgernote.com/columns/gigs-live-performance/stage-presence/

45. https://ledgernote.com/columns/gigs-live-performance/stage-presence/

46. https://ledgernote.com/columns/gigs-live-performance/stage-presence/

47. https://ledgernote.com/columns/gigs-live-performance/stage-presence/

48. https://ledgernote.com/columns/gigs-live-performance/stage-presence/

49. https://www.bbcmaestro.com/blog/what-is-stage-presence

Activities:

1. Performance Preparation:

○ **Traditional:** Prepare a live performance piece, incorporating stage presence, confidence, audience engagement, and choreography.

○ **VR:** Use VR platforms to prepare and rehearse a virtual live performance.

2. Live Performance:

○ **Traditional:** Perform the prepared piece in front of the class and discuss the experience.

○ **VR:** Use VR platforms to create and share virtual live performances.

3. Peer Feedback:

○ **Traditional:** Provide constructive feedback on each other's performances and discuss areas for improvement.

○ **VR:** Use VR collaboration tools to facilitate a virtual feedback session.

4. Case Study:

○ **Traditional:** Study the case of Prince, focusing on his live performances and stage presence.

○ **VR:** Use VR to explore virtual performances of Prince and discuss his stage presence techniques.

5. Reflection:

○ **Traditional:** Reflect on the live performance showcase and feedback activities and their impact on stage presence.

○ **VR:** Use VR journaling tools to reflect on the live performance experiences.

Week 24 Lesson Plans

Day 1: Exploring Identity and Self-Expression

Objective: Students will understand the importance of identity and self-expression and how to respect and celebrate diverse identities.

Activities:

- **Identity Exploration:**
  - **Traditional:** Discuss what identity means and why self-expression is important.
  - **VR:** Use VR platforms to explore different identities and self-expression in various cultures.

- **Self-Expression Activities:**

  o **Traditional:** Engage in activities that allow students to express their own identities, such as art or writing.

  o **VR:** Use VR tools to create virtual representations of their identities and share with the class.

- **Case Study:**

  o **Traditional:** Study the case of Frida Kahlo, focusing on how she expressed her identity through art.

  o **VR:** Use VR to explore virtual galleries of Frida Kahlo's work and discuss her self-expression.

- **Reflection:**

  o **Traditional:** Reflect on the identity and self-expression activities and their impact on understanding oneself and others.

  o **VR:** Use VR journaling tools to reflect on the identity exploration experiences.

Day 2: Empathy Through Literature

Objective: Students will learn to develop empathy by exploring characters and stories in literature.

Activities:

- **Literary Analysis:**
  - **Traditional:** Read and analyze stories or excerpts that highlight empathy and understanding.
  - **VR:** Use VR tools to immerse in the story settings and interact with characters.

- **Character Perspective:**
  - **Traditional:** Discuss the perspectives of different characters and their experiences.
  - **VR:** Use VR platforms to experience the story from the viewpoint of different characters.

- **Case Study:**
  - **Traditional:** Study the case of Harper Lee's "To Kill a Mockingbird," focusing on themes of empathy and justice.
  - **VR:** Use VR to explore virtual environments related to the story and discuss its impact.

- **Reflection:**
  - **Traditional:** Reflect on the literary analysis activities and their impact on understanding empathy.
  - **VR:** Use VR journaling tools to reflect on the literary experiences.

Day 3: Conflict Resolution and Mediation

Objective: Students will learn techniques for resolving conflicts and mediating disputes empathetically.

Activities:

- **Conflict Resolution Techniques:**
  - **Traditional:** Teach techniques for resolving conflicts, such as active listening and finding common ground.
  - **VR:** Use VR tools to simulate conflict scenarios and practice resolution techniques.

- **Mediation Practice:**

  - **Traditional:** Engage in role-playing exercises to practice mediation and conflict resolution.
  - **VR:** Use VR platforms to simulate mediation sessions and practice empathetic responses.

- **Case Study:**

  - **Traditional:** Study the case of Mahatma Gandhi, focusing on his non-violent approach to conflict resolution.
  - **VR:** Use VR to explore virtual environments related to Gandhi's work and discuss his techniques.

- **Reflection:**

  - **Traditional:** Reflect on the conflict resolution activities and their impact on understanding and resolving disputes.
  - **VR:** Use VR journaling tools to reflect on the mediation experiences.

Day 4: Empathy in Action

Objective: Students will apply empathy in real-world scenarios and community projects.

Activities:

- **Community Project Planning:**
  - **Traditional:** Plan a community project that promotes empathy and inclusion.
  - **VR:** Use VR tools to visualize and design the community project.

- **Empathy in Practice:**

  - **Traditional:** Engage in activities that put empathy into action, such as volunteering or community service.
  - **VR:** Use VR platforms to simulate community service activities and practice empathy.

- **Case Study:**

  - **Traditional:** Study the case of Mother Teresa, focusing on her empathetic approach to helping others.
  - **VR:** Use VR to explore virtual environments related to Mother Teresa's work and discuss her impact.

- **Reflection:**

  - **Traditional:** Reflect on the empathy in action activities and their impact on the community.
  - **VR:** Use VR journaling tools to reflect on the community project experiences.

Week 25 Lesson Plans

Day 1: Understanding Privilege and Equity

Objective: Students will learn about privilege and equity and how to recognize and address inequalities.

Activities:

- **Privilege Exploration:**
  - **Traditional:** Discuss what privilege is and how it affects different people in society.
  - **VR:** Use VR platforms to experience scenarios that highlight privilege and inequity.

- **Equity Exercises:**

  ○ **Traditional:** Engage in activities that illustrate the difference between equality and equity.
  - **VR:** Use VR tools to simulate situations where students can practice creating equitable solutions.

- **Case Study:**

  ○ **Traditional:** Study the case of Martin Luther King Jr., focusing on his fight for equity and civil rights.
  - **VR:** Use VR to explore virtual environments related to Martin Luther King Jr.'s work and discuss his impact.

- **Reflection:**

  ○ **Traditional:** Reflect on the privilege and equity activities and their impact on understanding societal inequalities.
  - **VR:** Use VR journaling tools to reflect on the privilege and equity experiences.

Day 2: Empathy in Leadership

Objective: Students will learn how empathy plays a crucial role in effective leadership.

Activities:

- **Leadership Qualities:**
  - ○ **Traditional:** Discuss the qualities of empathetic leaders and why empathy is important in leadership.
  - ○ **VR:** Use VR tools to explore examples of empathetic leadership in various settings.

- **Leadership Practice:**
  - ○ **Traditional:** Engage in activities that allow students to practice empathetic leadership, such as group projects.
  - ○ **VR:** Use VR platforms to simulate leadership scenarios and practice empathetic decision-making.

- **Case Study:**
  - ○ **Traditional:** Study the case of Jacinda Ardern, focusing on her empathetic leadership style.
  - ○ **VR:** Use VR to explore virtual environments related to Jacinda Ardern's work and discuss her leadership techniques.

- **Reflection:**
  - ○ **Traditional:** Reflect on the leadership activities and their impact on understanding empathetic leadership.
  - ○ **VR:** Use VR journaling tools to reflect on the leadership experiences.

Day 3: Empathy and Technology

Objective: Students will explore how technology can be used to foster empathy and inclusion.

Activities:

- **Technology Exploration:**
  - **Traditional:** Discuss how technology can be used to promote empathy and inclusion.
  - **VR:** Use VR tools to explore technological innovations that foster empathy, such as VR empathy simulations.

- ## Tech for Good Projects:

  - **Traditional:** Engage in projects that use technology to address social issues and promote empathy.
  - **VR:** Use VR platforms to design and implement tech-based solutions for fostering empathy and inclusion.

- ## Case Study:

  - **Traditional:** Study the case of the "Be My Eyes" app, focusing on how it uses technology to help visually impaired individuals.
  - **VR:** Use VR to explore virtual environments related to the app and discuss its impact.

- ## Reflection:

  - **Traditional:** Reflect on the technology activities and their impact on understanding the role of tech in empathy.
  - **VR:** Use VR journaling tools to reflect on the tech for good experiences.

Day 4: Empathy in Global Citizenship

Objective: Students will learn about global citizenship and how empathy can help address global challenges.

Activities:

• **Global Citizenship Exploration:**

○ **Traditional:** Discuss what it means to be a global citizen and the importance of empathy in global contexts.

○ **VR:** Use VR platforms to explore global issues and the role of empathy in addressing them.

• **Global Challenges Activities:**

○ **Traditional:** Engage in activities that address global challenges, such as climate change or poverty.

○ **VR:** Use VR tools to simulate global scenarios and practice empathetic problem-solving.

• **Case Study:**

○ **Traditional:** Study the case of Malala Yousafzai, focusing on her role as a global citizen and advocate for education.

○ **VR:** Use VR to explore virtual environments related to Malala's work and discuss her impact.

• **Reflection:**

○ **Traditional:** Reflect on the global citizenship activities and their impact on understanding global empathy.

○ **VR:** Use VR journaling tools to reflect on the global citizenship experiences.

Week 26 Lesson Plans

Day 1: Exploring Intersectionality

Objective: Students will understand the concept of intersectionality and how overlapping identities impact experiences.

Activities:

- **Intersectionality Exploration:**
  - **Traditional:** Discuss what intersectionality is and why it's important to consider multiple aspects of identity.
  - **VR:** Use VR platforms to explore scenarios that highlight intersectionality and its effects on individuals.

- **Identity Mapping:**

  - **Traditional:** Create identity maps that illustrate the different aspects of students' identities.
  - **VR:** Use VR tools to create virtual identity maps and share them with the class.

- **Case Study:**

  - **Traditional:** Study the case of Kimberlé Crenshaw, focusing on her work on intersectionality.
  - **VR:** Use VR to explore virtual environments related to Crenshaw's work and discuss her impact.

- **Reflection:**

  - **Traditional:** Reflect on the intersectionality activities and their impact on understanding diverse experiences.
  - **VR:** Use VR journaling tools to reflect on the intersectionality experiences.

Day 2: Empathy in Digital Spaces

Objective: Students will learn how to practice empathy and respect in online interactions.

Activities:

- **Digital Empathy Techniques:**
  - **Traditional:** Discuss techniques for practicing empathy and respect in digital communications.
  - **VR:** Use VR tools to simulate online interactions and practice empathetic responses.

Online Role-Playing:

- **Traditional:** Engage in role-playing exercises that simulate online scenarios requiring empathy.
- **VR:** Use VR platforms to create and participate in virtual role-playing activities.

Case Study:

- **Traditional:** Study the case of online communities that foster empathy and support, such as mental health forums.
- **VR:** Use VR to explore virtual environments of supportive online communities and discuss their impact.

Reflection:

- **Traditional:** Reflect on the digital empathy activities and their impact on online interactions.
- **VR:** Use VR journaling tools to reflect on the digital empathy experiences.

Day 3: Empathy and Environmental Stewardship

Objective: Students will learn about the connection between empathy and environmental stewardship.

Activities:

● **Environmental Empathy Exploration:**

  ○ **Traditional:** Discuss how empathy can drive environmental stewardship and the importance of caring for the planet.

  ○ **VR:** Use VR tools to explore environmental issues and the impact of human actions on the environment.

● **Stewardship Projects:**

  ○ **Traditional:** Plan and engage in projects that promote environmental stewardship, such as clean-up activities.

  ○ **VR:** Use VR platforms to simulate environmental projects and visualize their impact.

● **Case Study:**

  ○ **Traditional:** Study the case of Greta Thunberg, focusing on her advocacy for the environment.

  ○ **VR:** Use VR to explore virtual environments related to Greta Thunberg's work and discuss her impact.

● **Reflection:**

  ○ **Traditional:** Reflect on the environmental empathy activities and their impact on understanding stewardship.

  ○ **VR:** Use VR journaling tools to reflect on the environmental stewardship experiences.

Day 4: Empathy in Historical Contexts

Objective: Students will explore historical events through the lens of empathy to understand their impact on people.

Activities:

- **Historical Empathy Exploration:**
    - **Traditional:** Discuss how empathy can help us understand historical events and their impact on individuals and communities.
    - **VR:** Use VR tools to immerse in historical events and experience them from different perspectives.

Historical Role-Playing:

- **Traditional:** Engage in role-playing exercises that simulate historical scenarios requiring empathy.
    - **VR:** Use VR platforms to create and participate in virtual historical role-playing activities.

Case Study:

- **Traditional:** Study the case of the Civil Rights Movement, focusing on the experiences of those involved.
    - **VR:** Use VR to explore virtual environments related to the Civil Rights Movement and discuss its impact.

Reflection:

- **Traditional:** Reflect on the historical empathy activities and their impact on understanding history.
    - **VR:** Use VR journaling tools to reflect on the historical empathy experiences.

Week 27 Lesson Plans

Day 1: Empathy in Healthcare

Objective: Students will learn about the role of empathy in healthcare and how it impacts patient care.

Activities:

- **Healthcare Empathy Exploration:**
  - **Traditional:** Discuss the importance of empathy in healthcare and how it affects patient outcomes.
  - **VR:** Use VR platforms to simulate healthcare scenarios and observe empathetic interactions between healthcare providers and patients.

Role-Playing Scenarios:

- **Traditional:** Engage in role-playing exercises to practice empathetic communication in healthcare settings.
  - **VR:** Use VR tools to simulate patient-provider interactions and practice empathy.

Case Study:

- **Traditional:** Study the case of Florence Nightingale, focusing on her empathetic approach to nursing.
  - **VR:** Use VR to explore virtual environments related to Florence Nightingale's work and discuss her impact.

Reflection:

- **Traditional:** Reflect on the healthcare empathy activities and their impact on understanding patient care.

○ **VR:** Use VR journaling tools to reflect on the healthcare empathy experiences.

Day 2: Empathy in Education

Objective: Students will explore how empathy can enhance teaching and learning experiences.

Activities:

- **Educational Empathy Techniques:**

  ○ **Traditional:** Discuss techniques for incorporating empathy into teaching practices.

  ○ **VR:** Use VR tools to observe and practice empathetic teaching methods in virtual classrooms.

- **Interactive Teaching:**

  ○ **Traditional:** Engage in activities that allow students to practice empathetic teaching, such as peer tutoring.

  ○ **VR:** Use VR platforms to simulate teaching scenarios and practice empathy.

- **Case Study:**

  ○ **Traditional:** Study the case of Maria Montessori, focusing on her empathetic approach to education.

  ○ **VR:** Use VR to explore virtual environments related to Maria Montessori's work and discuss her techniques.

- **Reflection:**

  ○ **Traditional:** Reflect on the educational empathy activities and their impact on teaching and learning.

  ○ **VR:** Use VR journaling tools to reflect on the educational empathy experiences.

Day 3: Empathy in the Workplace

Objective: Students will learn about the importance of empathy in the workplace and how it can improve teamwork and productivity.

Activities:

- **Workplace Empathy Exploration:**
  - **Traditional:** Discuss the role of empathy in the workplace and its benefits for teamwork and productivity.
  - **VR:** Use VR tools to simulate workplace scenarios and observe empathetic interactions.

- **Team-Building Exercises:**
  - **Traditional:** Engage in team-building activities that promote empathy and collaboration.
  - **VR:** Use VR platforms to simulate team-building exercises and practice empathetic teamwork.

- **Case Study:**
  - **Traditional:** Study the case of Satya Nadella, focusing on his empathetic leadership at Microsoft.
  - **VR:** Use VR to explore virtual environments related to Satya Nadella's work and discuss his leadership style.

- **Reflection:**
  - **Traditional:** Reflect on the workplace empathy activities and their impact on teamwork and productivity.
  - **VR:** Use VR journaling tools to reflect on the workplace empathy experiences.

Day 4: Empathy in Media and Entertainment

Objective: Students will explore how empathy is portrayed in media and entertainment and its impact on audiences.

Activities:

- **Media Empathy Analysis:**
  - **Traditional:** Discuss how empathy is portrayed in various forms of media and its impact on audiences.
  - **VR:** Use VR tools to explore media content that highlights empathetic themes.

- **Creative Projects:**
  - **Traditional:** Engage in creative projects that involve producing media content with empathetic messages.
  - **VR:** Use VR platforms to create and share virtual media projects that promote empathy.

- **Case Study:**
  - **Traditional:** Study the case of Oprah Winfrey, focusing on her use of media to promote empathy and understanding.
  - **VR:** Use VR to explore virtual environments related to Oprah Winfrey's work and discuss her impact.

- **Reflection:**
  - **Traditional:** Reflect on the media empathy activities and their impact on understanding and promoting empathy.
  - **VR:** Use VR journaling tools to reflect on the media empathy experiences.

Week 28 Lesson Plans

Day 1: Empathy in Conflict Resolution

Objective: Students will learn advanced techniques for resolving conflicts empathetically and effectively.

Activities:

- **Advanced Conflict Resolution Techniques:**
  - **Traditional:** Discuss advanced techniques for resolving conflicts, such as negotiation and mediation.
  - **VR:** Use VR tools to simulate complex conflict scenarios and practice resolution techniques.

Mediation Role-Playing:

- **Traditional:** Engage in role-playing exercises to practice mediation and conflict resolution in challenging situations.
  - **VR:** Use VR platforms to simulate mediation sessions and practice empathetic responses.

Case Study:

- **Traditional:** Study the case of Desmond Tutu, focusing on his role in conflict resolution and reconciliation.
  - **VR:** Use VR to explore virtual environments related to Desmond Tutu's work and discuss his techniques.

Reflection:

- **Traditional:** Reflect on the conflict resolution activities and their impact on understanding and resolving disputes.
  - **VR:** Use VR journaling tools to reflect on the mediation experiences.

Day 2: Empathy in Social Justice

Objective: Students will explore the role of empathy in social justice movements and advocacy.

Activities:

● **Social Justice Exploration:**

  ○ **Traditional:** Discuss the importance of empathy in social justice and how it drives advocacy.

  ○ **VR:** Use VR tools to explore social justice movements and observe empathetic advocacy.

● **Advocacy Projects:**

○ **Traditional:** Plan and engage in projects that promote social justice and empathy.

  ○ **VR:** Use VR platforms to design and implement advocacy projects in virtual environments.

● **Case Study:**

○ **Traditional:** Study the case of Rosa Parks, focusing on her role in the Civil Rights Movement and her empathetic advocacy.

  ○ **VR:** Use VR to explore virtual environments related to Rosa Parks' work and discuss her impact.

● **Reflection:**

○ **Traditional:** Reflect on the social justice activities and their impact on understanding and promoting empathy.

  ○ **VR:** Use VR journaling tools to reflect on the social justice experiences.

Day 3: Empathy in Art and Creativity

Objective: Students will explore how empathy can be expressed through art and creative projects.

Activities:

- **Creative Empathy Exploration:**
  - **Traditional:** Discuss how empathy can be expressed through various forms of art and creativity.
  - **VR:** Use VR tools to explore artistic expressions of empathy in virtual galleries and exhibitions.

Art Projects:

- **Traditional:** Engage in art projects that focus on expressing empathy, such as painting, sculpture, or digital art.
- **VR:** Use VR platforms to create and share virtual art projects that promote empathy.

Case Study:

- **Traditional:** Study the case of Vincent van Gogh, focusing on how his art expressed his emotions and empathy.
- **VR:** Use VR to explore virtual galleries of van Gogh's work and discuss his artistic expression.

Reflection:

- **Traditional:** Reflect on the creative empathy activities and their impact on understanding and expressing empathy.
- **VR:** Use VR journaling tools to reflect on the artistic experiences.

Day 4: Empathy in Sports and Teamwork

Objective: Students will learn about the role of empathy in sports and how it enhances teamwork and sportsmanship.

Activities:

- **Sports Empathy Exploration:**
  - **Traditional:** Discuss the importance of empathy in sports and how it contributes to teamwork and sportsmanship.
  - **VR:** Use VR tools to simulate sports scenarios and observe empathetic interactions among teammates.

- **Team-Building Sports Activities:**

  - **Traditional:** Engage in sports activities that promote empathy and teamwork, such as cooperative games.
  - **VR:** Use VR platforms to simulate team sports and practice empathetic teamwork.

- **Case Study:**

  - **Traditional:** Study the case of Jackie Robinson, focusing on his role in breaking racial barriers in sports and his empathetic approach.
  - **VR:** Use VR to explore virtual environments related to Jackie Robinson's career and discuss his impact.

- **Reflection:**

  - **Traditional:** Reflect on the sports empathy activities and their impact on understanding teamwork and sportsmanship.
  - **VR:** Use VR journaling tools to reflect on the sports experiences.

Week 29 Lesson Plans

Day 1: Empathy in Law and Justice

Objective: Students will learn about the role of empathy in the legal system and how it impacts justice and fairness.

Activities:

- **Legal Empathy Exploration:**
  - **Traditional:** Discuss the importance of empathy in the legal system and how it affects justice and fairness.
  - **VR:** Use VR tools to simulate courtroom scenarios and observe empathetic interactions between legal professionals and clients.

- **Mock Trials:**

  - **Traditional:** Engage in mock trial exercises to practice empathetic communication and decision-making in legal contexts.
  - **VR:** Use VR platforms to simulate trial scenarios and practice empathy in legal settings.

- **Case Study:**

  - **Traditional:** Study the case of Ruth Bader Ginsburg, focusing on her empathetic approach to justice and equality.
  - **VR:** Use VR to explore virtual environments related to Ruth Bader Ginsburg's work and discuss her impact.

- **Reflection:**

  - **Traditional:** Reflect on the legal empathy activities and their impact on understanding justice and fairness.
  - **VR:** Use VR journaling tools to reflect on the legal empathy experiences.

Day 2: Empathy in Crisis Situations

Objective: Students will learn how to apply empathy in crisis situations and provide support to those in need.

Activities:

- **Crisis Empathy Techniques:**
  - **Traditional:** Discuss techniques for providing empathetic support in crisis situations, such as active listening and emotional validation.
  - **VR:** Use VR tools to simulate crisis scenarios and practice empathetic responses.

- **Crisis Response Role-Playing:**

  - **Traditional:** Engage in role-playing exercises to practice providing support in various crisis situations.
  - **VR:** Use VR platforms to simulate crisis response scenarios and practice empathy.

- **Case Study:**

  - **Traditional:** Study the case of the Red Cross, focusing on their empathetic approach to disaster relief and support.
  - **VR:** Use VR to explore virtual environments related to the Red Cross's work and discuss their impact.

- **Reflection:**

  - **Traditional:** Reflect on the crisis empathy activities and their impact on understanding and providing support.
  - **VR:** Use VR journaling tools to reflect on the crisis response experiences.

Day 3: Empathy in Cultural Exchange

Objective: Students will explore the role of empathy in cultural exchange and understanding different perspectives.

Activities:

- **Cultural Exchange Exploration:**
  - **Traditional:** Discuss the importance of empathy in cultural exchange and how it fosters understanding and respect.
  - **VR:** Use VR tools to explore different cultures and observe empathetic interactions in cultural exchanges.

- **Cultural Exchange Activities:**
  - **Traditional:** Engage in activities that promote cultural exchange, such as sharing cultural traditions and stories.
  - **VR:** Use VR platforms to simulate cultural exchange scenarios and practice empathy.

- **Case Study:**
  - **Traditional:** Study the case of the Peace Corps, focusing on their role in promoting cultural exchange and empathy.
  - **VR:** Use VR to explore virtual environments related to the Peace Corps's work and discuss their impact.

- **Reflection:**
  - **Traditional:** Reflect on the cultural exchange activities and their impact on understanding and respecting different perspectives.
  - **VR:** Use VR journaling tools to reflect on the cultural exchange experiences.

Day 4: Empathy in Personal Growth

Objective: Students will learn how empathy contributes to personal growth and self-awareness.

Activities:

- **Personal Growth Exploration:**
   - **Traditional:** Discuss how empathy contributes to personal growth and self-awareness.
   - **VR:** Use VR tools to explore scenarios that highlight the role of empathy in personal development.

- ## Self-Reflection Activities:

   - **Traditional:** Engage in activities that promote self-reflection and empathy, such as journaling and mindfulness exercises.
   - **VR:** Use VR platforms to create virtual self-reflection experiences and practice empathy.

- ## Case Study:

   - **Traditional:** Study the case of Brené Brown, focusing on her work on vulnerability, empathy, and personal growth.
   - **VR:** Use VR to explore virtual environments related to Brené Brown's work and discuss her impact.

- ## Reflection:

   - **Traditional:** Reflect on the personal growth activities and their impact on understanding and practicing empathy.
   - **VR:** Use VR journaling tools to reflect on the personal growth experiences.

Week 30 Lesson Plans

Day 1: Empathy in Politics and Governance

Objective: Students will learn about the role of empathy in politics and governance and how it influences policy-making.

Activities:

- **Political Empathy Exploration:**

  ○ **Traditional:** Discuss the importance of empathy in politics and how it affects policy-making and governance.

  ○ **VR:** Use VR tools to simulate political scenarios and observe empathetic interactions between politicians and constituents.

- **Policy-Making Role-Playing:**

○ **Traditional:** Engage in role-playing exercises to practice empathetic decision-making in political contexts.

  ○ **VR:** Use VR platforms to simulate policy-making scenarios and practice empathy in governance.

- **Case Study:**

○ **Traditional:** Study the case of Nelson Mandela, focusing on his empathetic approach to leadership and governance.

  ○ **VR:** Use VR to explore virtual environments related to Nelson Mandela's work and discuss his impact.

- **Reflection:**

○ **Traditional:** Reflect on the political empathy activities and their impact on understanding governance and policy-making.

  ○ **VR:** Use VR journaling tools to reflect on the political empathy experiences.

Day 2: Empathy in Business and Entrepreneurship

Objective: Students will explore how empathy can drive innovation and success in business and entrepreneurship.

Activities:

- **Business Empathy Techniques:**
  - **Traditional:** Discuss the role of empathy in business and how it can lead to better customer relations and innovation.
  - **VR:** Use VR tools to simulate business scenarios and observe empathetic interactions with customers and employees.

- **Entrepreneurship Projects:**

  - **Traditional:** Plan and engage in projects that incorporate empathy into business models and customer service.
  - **VR:** Use VR platforms to design and implement business projects that promote empathy.

- **Case Study:**

  - **Traditional:** Study the case of Howard Schultz, focusing on his empathetic approach to leadership at Starbucks.
  - **VR:** Use VR to explore virtual environments related to Howard Schultz's work and discuss his impact.

- **Reflection:**

  - **Traditional:** Reflect on the business empathy activities and their impact on understanding entrepreneurship and customer relations.
  - **VR:** Use VR journaling tools to reflect on the business empathy experiences.

Day 3: Empathy in Science and Research

Objective: Students will learn about the role of empathy in scientific research and how it influences ethical considerations.

Activities:

- **Scientific Empathy Exploration:**
  - **Traditional:** Discuss the importance of empathy in scientific research and how it affects ethical decision-making.
  - **VR:** Use VR tools to simulate research scenarios and observe empathetic interactions in scientific contexts.

- **Ethical Dilemmas:**

  - **Traditional:** Engage in discussions and activities that explore ethical dilemmas in scientific research.
  - **VR:** Use VR platforms to simulate ethical decision-making scenarios in research.

- **Case Study:**

  - **Traditional:** Study the case of Jane Goodall, focusing on her empathetic approach to animal research and conservation.
  - **VR:** Use VR to explore virtual environments related to Jane Goodall's work and discuss her impact.

- **Reflection:**

  - **Traditional:** Reflect on the scientific empathy activities and their impact on understanding ethical research.
  - **VR:** Use VR journaling tools to reflect on the scientific empathy experiences.

Day 4: Empathy in Literature and Writing

Objective: Students will explore how empathy is expressed in literature and how it enhances storytelling.

Activities:

- **Literary Empathy Analysis:**
  ○ **Traditional:** Discuss how empathy is portrayed in literature and its impact on readers.
  ○ **VR:** Use VR tools to immerse in literary settings and interact with characters to understand their perspectives.

- **Creative Writing Projects:**

  ○ **Traditional:** Engage in creative writing projects that focus on expressing empathy through storytelling.
  ○ **VR:** Use VR platforms to create and share virtual stories that highlight empathetic themes.

- **Case Study:**

  ○ **Traditional:** Study the case of J.K. Rowling, focusing on how her writing in the Harry Potter series promotes empathy and understanding.
  ○ **VR:** Use VR to explore virtual environments related to the Harry Potter series and discuss its impact.

- **Reflection:**

  ○ **Traditional:** Reflect on the literary empathy activities and their impact on understanding and expressing empathy.
  ○ **VR:** Use VR journaling tools to reflect on the literary empathy experiences.

Week 31 Lesson Plans

Day 1: Empathy in Journalism and Media

Objective: Students will learn about the role of empathy in journalism and how it influences storytelling and reporting.

Activities:

- **Journalistic Empathy Exploration:**
  - **Traditional:** Discuss the importance of empathy in journalism and how it affects storytelling and reporting.
  - **VR:** Use VR tools to simulate journalistic scenarios and observe empathetic interactions between journalists and their subjects.

- **Reporting Role-Playing:**

  - **Traditional:** Engage in role-playing exercises to practice empathetic interviewing and reporting techniques.
  - **VR:** Use VR platforms to simulate reporting scenarios and practice empathy in journalism.

- **Case Study:**

  - **Traditional:** Study the case of Christiane Amanpour, focusing on her empathetic approach to international reporting.
  - **VR:** Use VR to explore virtual environments related to Christiane Amanpour's work and discuss her impact.

- **Reflection:**

  - **Traditional:** Reflect on the journalistic empathy activities and their impact on understanding storytelling and reporting.
  - **VR:** Use VR journaling tools to reflect on the journalistic empathy experiences.

Day 2: Empathy in Community Service

Objective: Students will explore the role of empathy in community service and how it fosters social responsibility.

Activities:

- **Community Service Exploration:**
  - **Traditional:** Discuss the importance of empathy in community service and how it fosters social responsibility.
  - **VR:** Use VR tools to simulate community service scenarios and observe empathetic interactions.

- **Service Projects:**
  - **Traditional:** Plan and engage in community service projects that promote empathy and social responsibility.
  - **VR:** Use VR platforms to design and implement virtual community service projects.

- **Case Study:**
  - **Traditional:** Study the case of Habitat for Humanity, focusing on their empathetic approach to building communities.
  - **VR:** Use VR to explore virtual environments related to Habitat for Humanity's work and discuss their impact.

- **Reflection:**
  - **Traditional:** Reflect on the community service activities and their impact on understanding social responsibility.
  - **VR:** Use VR journaling tools to reflect on the community service experiences.

Day 3: Empathy in Technology Design

Objective: Students will learn about the role of empathy in technology design and how it influences user experience.

Activities:

- **Tech Design Empathy Exploration:**
  - **Traditional:** Discuss the importance of empathy in technology design and how it affects user experience.
  - **VR:** Use VR tools to explore examples of empathetic technology design and observe user interactions.

- **Design Thinking Projects:**

  - **Traditional:** Engage in design thinking projects that focus on creating empathetic technology solutions.
  - **VR:** Use VR platforms to design and prototype virtual technology solutions that promote empathy.

- **Case Study:**

  - **Traditional:** Study the case of IDEO, focusing on their empathetic approach to design thinking and innovation.
  - **VR:** Use VR to explore virtual environments related to IDEO's work and discuss their impact.

- **Reflection:**

  - **Traditional:** Reflect on the tech design empathy activities and their impact on understanding user experience.
  - **VR:** Use VR journaling tools to reflect on the tech design experiences.

Day 4: Empathy in Performing Arts

Objective: Students will explore how empathy is expressed in performing arts and its impact on audiences.

Activities:

- **Performing Arts Empathy Exploration:**
  - **Traditional:** Discuss how empathy is expressed in performing arts and its impact on audiences.
  - **VR:** Use VR tools to explore performances that highlight empathetic themes and observe audience reactions.

Performance Projects:

- **Traditional:** Engage in performing arts projects that focus on expressing empathy, such as theater or dance.
  - **VR:** Use VR platforms to create and share virtual performances that promote empathy.

Case Study:

- **Traditional:** Study the case of Lin-Manuel Miranda, focusing on how his work in "Hamilton" promotes empathy and understanding.
  - **VR:** Use VR to explore virtual environments related to "Hamilton" and discuss its impact.

Reflection:

- **Traditional:** Reflect on the performing arts empathy activities and their impact on understanding and expressing empathy.
  - **VR:** Use VR journaling tools to reflect on the performing arts experiences.

Week 32 Lesson Plans

Day 1: Empathy in Environmental Advocacy

Objective: Students will learn about the role of empathy in environmental advocacy and how it drives conservation efforts.

Activities:

- **Environmental Empathy Exploration:**
  - **Traditional:** Discuss the importance of empathy in environmental advocacy and how it influences conservation efforts.
  - **VR:** Use VR tools to explore environmental issues and observe empathetic interactions in advocacy campaigns.

- **Advocacy Projects:**

  - **Traditional:** Plan and engage in projects that promote environmental conservation and empathy.
  - **VR:** Use VR platforms to design and implement virtual advocacy projects for environmental issues.

- **Case Study:**

  - **Traditional:** Study the case of Wangari Maathai, focusing on her empathetic approach to environmental conservation.
  - **VR:** Use VR to explore virtual environments related to Wangari Maathai's work and discuss her impact.

- **Reflection:**

  - **Traditional:** Reflect on the environmental advocacy activities and their impact on understanding conservation.
  - **VR:** Use VR journaling tools to reflect on the environmental advocacy experiences.

Day 2: Empathy in Family Dynamics

Objective: Students will explore the role of empathy in family relationships and how it strengthens family bonds.

Activities:

- **Family Empathy Exploration:**
  - **Traditional:** Discuss the importance of empathy in family dynamics and how it strengthens relationships.
  - **VR:** Use VR tools to simulate family scenarios and observe empathetic interactions.

- **Family Role-Playing:**

  - **Traditional:** Engage in role-playing exercises to practice empathetic communication within family settings.
  - **VR:** Use VR platforms to simulate family interactions and practice empathy.

- **Case Study:**

  - **Traditional:** Study the case of Michelle Obama, focusing on her empathetic approach to family and community.
  - **VR:** Use VR to explore virtual environments related to Michelle Obama's work and discuss her impact.

- **Reflection:**

  - **Traditional:** Reflect on the family empathy activities and their impact on understanding family dynamics.
  - **VR:** Use VR journaling tools to reflect on the family empathy experiences.

Day 3: Empathy in Peer Relationships

Objective: Students will learn about the role of empathy in peer relationships and how it fosters mutual respect and understanding.

Activities:

- **Peer Empathy Exploration:**

   ○ **Traditional:** Discuss the importance of empathy in peer relationships and how it fosters mutual respect.

   ○ **VR:** Use VR tools to simulate peer interactions and observe empathetic communication.

- **Peer Role-Playing:**

○ **Traditional:** Engage in role-playing exercises to practice empathetic communication with peers.

   ○ **VR:** Use VR platforms to simulate peer interactions and practice empathy.

- **Case Study:**

○ **Traditional:** Study the case of Malala Yousafzai, focusing on her empathetic approach to peer relationships and advocacy.

   ○ **VR:** Use VR to explore virtual environments related to Malala Yousafzai's work and discuss her impact.

- **Reflection:**

○ **Traditional:** Reflect on the peer empathy activities and their impact on understanding peer relationships.

   ○ **VR:** Use VR journaling tools to reflect on the peer empathy experiences.

Day 4: Empathy in Global Health

Objective: Students will explore the role of empathy in global health initiatives and how it improves health outcomes.

Activities:

- **Global Health Empathy Exploration:**
    - **Traditional:** Discuss the importance of empathy in global health and how it improves health outcomes.
    - **VR:** Use VR tools to explore global health issues and observe empathetic interactions in health initiatives.

- **Health Advocacy Projects:**

    - **Traditional:** Plan and engage in projects that promote global health and empathy.
    - **VR:** Use VR platforms to design and implement virtual health advocacy projects.

- **Case Study:**

    - **Traditional:** Study the case of Paul Farmer, focusing on his empathetic approach to global health and healthcare delivery.
    - **VR:** Use VR to explore virtual environments related to Paul Farmer's work and discuss his impact.

- **Reflection:**

    - **Traditional:** Reflect on the global health empathy activities and their impact on understanding health initiatives.
    - **VR:** Use VR journaling tools to reflect on the global health experiences.

Week 33 Lesson Plans

Day 1: Empathy in Conflict Mediation

Objective: Students will learn advanced techniques for mediating conflicts empathetically and effectively.

Activities:

- **Conflict Mediation Techniques:**

    ○ **Traditional:** Discuss advanced techniques for mediating conflicts, such as active listening and finding common ground.

    ○ **VR:** Use VR tools to simulate complex conflict scenarios and practice mediation techniques.

- **Mediation Role-Playing:**

○ **Traditional:** Engage in role-playing exercises to practice mediation in challenging situations.

    ○ **VR:** Use VR platforms to simulate mediation sessions and practice empathetic responses.

- **Case Study:**

○ **Traditional:** Study the case of Kofi Annan, focusing on his role in conflict mediation and peacekeeping.

    ○ **VR:** Use VR to explore virtual environments related to Kofi Annan's work and discuss his techniques.

- **Reflection:**

○ **Traditional:** Reflect on the conflict mediation activities and their impact on understanding and resolving disputes.

    ○ **VR:** Use VR journaling tools to reflect on the mediation experiences.

Day 2: Empathy in Human Rights Advocacy

Objective: Students will explore the role of empathy in human rights advocacy and how it drives social change.

Activities:

- **Human Rights Exploration:**
  - **Traditional:** Discuss the importance of empathy in human rights advocacy and how it drives social change.
  - **VR:** Use VR tools to explore human rights issues and observe empathetic interactions in advocacy campaigns.

- **Advocacy Projects:**
  - **Traditional:** Plan and engage in projects that promote human rights and empathy.
  - **VR:** Use VR platforms to design and implement virtual advocacy projects for human rights issues.

- **Case Study:**
  - **Traditional:** Study the case of Eleanor Roosevelt, focusing on her empathetic approach to human rights advocacy.
  - **VR:** Use VR to explore virtual environments related to Eleanor Roosevelt's work and discuss her impact.

- **Reflection:**
  - **Traditional:** Reflect on the human rights advocacy activities and their impact on understanding social change.
  - **VR:** Use VR journaling tools to reflect on the human rights advocacy experiences.

Day 3: Empathy in Creative Writing

Objective: Students will explore how empathy can be expressed through creative writing and storytelling.

Activities:

- **Creative Writing Techniques:**
  - **Traditional:** Discuss techniques for expressing empathy through creative writing and storytelling.
  - **VR:** Use VR tools to create immersive storytelling experiences that highlight empathetic themes.

- **Writing Projects:**
  - **Traditional:** Engage in creative writing projects that focus on expressing empathy, such as short stories or poems.
  - **VR:** Use VR platforms to create and share virtual stories that promote empathy.

- **Case Study:**
  - **Traditional:** Study the case of Maya Angelou, focusing on how her writing expresses empathy and understanding.
  - **VR:** Use VR to explore virtual environments related to Maya Angelou's work and discuss her impact.

- **Reflection:**
  - **Traditional:** Reflect on the creative writing activities and their impact on understanding and expressing empathy.
  - **VR:** Use VR journaling tools to reflect on the creative writing experiences.

Day 4: Empathy in Global Citizenship

Objective: Students will learn about the role of empathy in global citizenship and how it helps address global challenges.

Activities:

- **Global Citizenship Exploration:**
  - **Traditional:** Discuss what it means to be a global citizen and the importance of empathy in global contexts.
  - **VR:** Use VR platforms to explore global issues and the role of empathy in addressing them.

- **Global Challenges Activities:**

  - **Traditional:** Engage in activities that address global challenges, such as climate change or poverty.
  - **VR:** Use VR tools to simulate global scenarios and practice empathetic problem-solving.

- **Case Study:**

  - **Traditional:** Study the case of Ban Ki-moon, focusing on his role as a global citizen and advocate for peace.
  - **VR:** Use VR to explore virtual environments related to Ban Ki-moon's work and discuss his impact.

- **Reflection:**

  - **Traditional:** Reflect on the global citizenship activities and their impact on understanding global empathy.
  - **VR:** Use VR journaling tools to reflect on the global citizenship experiences.

Week 34 Lesson Plans

Day 1: Empathy in Mental Health Support

Objective: Students will learn about the role of empathy in mental health support and how it improves well-being.

Activities:

- **Mental Health Empathy Exploration:**
  - **Traditional:** Discuss the importance of empathy in mental health support and how it improves well-being.
  - **VR:** Use VR tools to simulate mental health support scenarios and observe empathetic interactions.

- **Support Role-Playing:**

  o **Traditional:** Engage in role-playing exercises to practice empathetic communication in mental health support.
  - **VR:** Use VR platforms to simulate mental health support sessions and practice empathy.

- **Case Study:**

  o **Traditional:** Study the case of Dr. Carl Rogers, focusing on his empathetic approach to psychotherapy.
  - **VR:** Use VR to explore virtual environments related to Dr. Carl Rogers's work and discuss his impact.

- **Reflection:**

  o **Traditional:** Reflect on the mental health empathy activities and their impact on understanding and providing support.
  - **VR:** Use VR journaling tools to reflect on the mental health support experiences.

Day 2: Empathy in Social Media

Objective: Students will explore the role of empathy in social media interactions and how it fosters positive online communities.

Activities:

- **Social Media Empathy Exploration:**
  - **Traditional:** Discuss the importance of empathy in social media interactions and how it fosters positive online communities.
  - **VR:** Use VR tools to simulate social media scenarios and observe empathetic interactions.

Online Role-Playing:

  - **Traditional:** Engage in role-playing exercises to practice empathetic communication on social media.
  - **VR:** Use VR platforms to simulate social media interactions and practice empathy.

Case Study:

  - **Traditional:** Study the case of social media campaigns that promote empathy and kindness, such as the #ChooseKind campaign.
  - **VR:** Use VR to explore virtual environments related to these campaigns and discuss their impact.

Reflection:

  - **Traditional:** Reflect on the social media empathy activities and their impact on understanding online interactions.
  - **VR:** Use VR journaling tools to reflect on the social media empathy experiences.

Day 3: Empathy in Cultural Heritage

Objective: Students will learn about the role of empathy in preserving and respecting cultural heritage.

Activities:

- **Cultural Heritage Exploration:**
  - **Traditional:** Discuss the importance of empathy in preserving and respecting cultural heritage.
  - **VR:** Use VR tools to explore cultural heritage sites and observe empathetic interactions in preservation efforts.

- **Heritage Projects:**
  - **Traditional:** Plan and engage in projects that promote the preservation and respect of cultural heritage.
  - **VR:** Use VR platforms to design and implement virtual heritage preservation projects.

- **Case Study:**
  - **Traditional:** Study the case of UNESCO World Heritage Sites, focusing on their role in preserving cultural heritage.
  - **VR:** Use VR to explore virtual environments related to UNESCO World Heritage Sites and discuss their impact.

- **Reflection:**
  - **Traditional:** Reflect on the cultural heritage activities and their impact on understanding preservation.
  - **VR:** Use VR journaling tools to reflect on the cultural heritage experiences.

Day 4: Empathy in Scientific Discovery

Objective: Students will explore how empathy influences scientific discovery and collaboration.

Activities:

- **Scientific Empathy Exploration:**
  - ○ **Traditional:** Discuss the importance of empathy in scientific discovery and how it influences collaboration.
  - ○ **VR:** Use VR tools to simulate scientific research scenarios and observe empathetic interactions.

- ## Collaboration Projects:

  ○ **Traditional:** Engage in collaborative projects that focus on scientific discovery and empathy.
  - ○ **VR:** Use VR platforms to design and implement virtual scientific research projects.

- ## Case Study:

  ○ **Traditional:** Study the case of Rosalind Franklin, focusing on her contributions to the discovery of DNA and the importance of empathy in scientific collaboration.
  - ○ **VR:** Use VR to explore virtual environments related to Rosalind Franklin's work and discuss her impact.

- ## Reflection:

  ○ **Traditional:** Reflect on the scientific empathy activities and their impact on understanding discovery and collaboration.
  - ○ **VR:** Use VR journaling tools to reflect on the scientific discovery experiences.

Week 35 Lesson Plans

Day 1: Empathy in Crisis Management

Objective: Students will learn about the role of empathy in crisis management and how it helps in effective response and recovery.

Activities:

- **Crisis Management Empathy Exploration:**
  - **Traditional:** Discuss the importance of empathy in crisis management and how it aids in response and recovery.
  - **VR:** Use VR tools to simulate crisis scenarios and observe empathetic interactions in crisis management.

- **Crisis Response Role-Playing:**

  - **Traditional:** Engage in role-playing exercises to practice empathetic communication in crisis situations.
  - **VR:** Use VR platforms to simulate crisis response scenarios and practice empathy.

- **Case Study:**

  - **Traditional:** Study the case of the 2010 Haiti earthquake response, focusing on the empathetic approaches used in the recovery efforts.
  - **VR:** Use VR to explore virtual environments related to the Haiti earthquake response and discuss its impact.

- **Reflection:**

  - **Traditional:** Reflect on the crisis management empathy activities and their impact on understanding response and recovery.
  - **VR:** Use VR journaling tools to reflect on the crisis management experiences.

Day 2: Empathy in Artistic Expression

Objective: Students will explore how empathy can be expressed through various forms of art and its impact on audiences.

Activities:

● **Artistic Empathy Exploration:**

   ○ **Traditional:** Discuss how empathy can be expressed through different forms of art and its impact on audiences.

   ○ **VR:** Use VR tools to explore artistic expressions of empathy in virtual galleries and exhibitions.

● **Art Projects:**

○ **Traditional:** Engage in art projects that focus on expressing empathy, such as painting, sculpture, or digital art.

   ○ **VR:** Use VR platforms to create and share virtual art projects that promote empathy.

● **Case Study:**

○ **Traditional:** Study the case of Pablo Picasso, focusing on how his art expressed empathy and social commentary.

   ○ **VR:** Use VR to explore virtual galleries of Picasso's work and discuss his artistic expression.

● **Reflection:**

○ **Traditional:** Reflect on the artistic empathy activities and their impact on understanding and expressing empathy.

   ○ **VR:** Use VR journaling tools to reflect on the artistic experiences.

Day 3: Empathy in Sports Leadership

Objective: Students will learn about the role of empathy in sports leadership and how it enhances team dynamics and performance.

Activities:

- **Sports Leadership Empathy Exploration:**
  - **Traditional:** Discuss the importance of empathy in sports leadership and how it enhances team dynamics and performance.
  - **VR:** Use VR tools to simulate sports leadership scenarios and observe empathetic interactions among team members.

- **Leadership Role-Playing:**

  - **Traditional:** Engage in role-playing exercises to practice empathetic leadership in sports settings.
  - **VR:** Use VR platforms to simulate sports leadership scenarios and practice empathy.

- **Case Study:**

  - **Traditional:** Study the case of Billie Jean King, focusing on her empathetic approach to sports leadership and advocacy for equality.
  - **VR:** Use VR to explore virtual environments related to Billie Jean King's career and discuss her impact.

- **Reflection:**

  - **Traditional:** Reflect on the sports leadership empathy activities and their impact on understanding team dynamics and performance.
  - **VR:** Use VR journaling tools to reflect on the sports leadership experiences.

Day 4: Empathy in Historical Narratives

Objective: Students will explore how empathy can be used to understand and interpret historical events and narratives.

Activities:

- **Historical Empathy Exploration:**
  - **Traditional:** Discuss how empathy can be used to understand and interpret historical events and narratives.
  - **VR:** Use VR tools to immerse in historical events and experience them from different perspectives.

- **Historical Role-Playing:**

  - **Traditional:** Engage in role-playing exercises that simulate historical scenarios requiring empathy.
  - **VR:** Use VR platforms to create and participate in virtual historical role-playing activities.

- **Case Study:**

  - **Traditional:** Study the case of Anne Frank, focusing on her diary and the empathetic understanding of her experiences during the Holocaust.
  - **VR:** Use VR to explore virtual environments related to Anne Frank's life and discuss her impact.

- **Reflection:**

  - **Traditional:** Reflect on the historical empathy activities and their impact on understanding history.
  - **VR:** Use VR journaling tools to reflect on the historical empathy experiences.

Week 36 Lesson Plans

Day 1: Empathy in Conflict Resolution

Objective: Students will learn advanced techniques for resolving conflicts empathetically and effectively.

Activities:

- **Conflict Resolution Techniques:**
  - **Traditional:** Discuss advanced techniques for resolving conflicts, such as negotiation and mediation.
  - **VR:** Use VR tools to simulate complex conflict scenarios and practice resolution techniques.

- **Mediation Role-Playing:**

  - **Traditional:** Engage in role-playing exercises to practice mediation and conflict resolution in challenging situations.
  - **VR:** Use VR platforms to simulate mediation sessions and practice empathetic responses.

- **Case Study:**

  - **Traditional:** Study the case of Desmond Tutu, focusing on his role in conflict resolution and reconciliation.
  - **VR:** Use VR to explore virtual environments related to Desmond Tutu's work and discuss his techniques.

- **Reflection:**

  - **Traditional:** Reflect on the conflict resolution activities and their impact on understanding and resolving disputes.
  - **VR:** Use VR journaling tools to reflect on the mediation experiences.

Day 2: Empathy in Social Justice

Objective: Students will explore the role of empathy in social justice movements and advocacy.

Activities:

- **Social Justice Exploration:**

  ○ **Traditional:** Discuss the importance of empathy in social justice and how it drives advocacy.

  ○ **VR:** Use VR tools to explore social justice movements and observe empathetic advocacy.

- **Advocacy Projects:**

  ○ **Traditional:** Plan and engage in projects that promote social justice and empathy.

  ○ **VR:** Use VR platforms to design and implement advocacy projects in virtual environments.

- **Case Study:**

  ○ **Traditional:** Study the case of Rosa Parks, focusing on her role in the Civil Rights Movement and her empathetic advocacy.

  ○ **VR:** Use VR to explore virtual environments related to Rosa Parks' work and discuss her impact.

- **Reflection:**

  ○ **Traditional:** Reflect on the social justice activities and their impact on understanding and promoting empathy.

  ○ **VR:** Use VR journaling tools to reflect on the social justice experiences.

Day 3: Empathy in Creative Writing

Objective: Students will explore how empathy can be expressed through creative writing and storytelling.

Activities:

- **Creative Writing Techniques:**
  - **Traditional:** Discuss techniques for expressing empathy through creative writing and storytelling.
  - **VR:** Use VR tools to create immersive storytelling experiences that highlight empathetic themes.

- **Writing Projects:**

  - **Traditional:** Engage in creative writing projects that focus on expressing empathy, such as short stories or poems.
  - **VR:** Use VR platforms to create and share virtual stories that promote empathy.

- **Case Study:**

  - **Traditional:** Study the case of Maya Angelou, focusing on how her writing expresses empathy and understanding.
  - **VR:** Use VR to explore virtual environments related to Maya Angelou's work and discuss her impact.

- **Reflection:**

  - **Traditional:** Reflect on the creative writing activities and their impact on understanding and expressing empathy.
  - **VR:** Use VR journaling tools to reflect on the creative writing experiences.

Day 4: Empathy in Global Citizenship

Objective: Students will learn about the role of empathy in global citizenship and how it helps address global challenges.

Activities:

- **Global Citizenship Exploration:**
  - **Traditional:** Discuss what it means to be a global citizen and the importance of empathy in global contexts.
  - **VR:** Use VR platforms to explore global issues and the role of empathy in addressing them.

- **Global Challenges Activities:**

  - **Traditional:** Engage in activities that address global challenges, such as climate change or poverty.
  - **VR:** Use VR tools to simulate global scenarios and practice empathetic problem-solving.

- **Case Study:**

  - **Traditional:** Study the case of Ban Ki-moon, focusing on his role as a global citizen and advocate for peace.
  - **VR:** Use VR to explore virtual environments related to Ban Ki-moon's work and discuss his impact.

- **Reflection:**

  - **Traditional:** Reflect on the global citizenship activities and their impact on understanding global empathy.
  - **VR:** Use VR journaling tools to reflect on the global citizenship experiences.

Week 37 Lesson Plans

Day 1: Sensory Empathy in Everyday Interactions

Objective: Students will learn about sensory empathy and how it enhances everyday interactions.

Activities:

- **Sensory Empathy Exploration:**
  - **Traditional:** Discuss the concept of sensory empathy and how it enhances understanding in everyday interactions.
  - **VR:** Use VR tools to simulate scenarios where sensory empathy is crucial, such as understanding sensory overload in crowded places.

- **Role-Playing Exercises:**

  - **Traditional:** Engage in role-playing exercises to practice sensory empathy in various everyday situations.
  - **VR:** Use VR platforms to simulate sensory experiences and practice empathetic responses.

- **Case Study:**

  - **Traditional:** Study the case of Temple Grandin, focusing on her insights into sensory experiences and empathy.
  - **VR:** Use VR to explore virtual environments related to Temple Grandin's work and discuss her impact.

- **Reflection:**

  - **Traditional:** Reflect on the sensory empathy activities and their impact on understanding everyday interactions.
  - **VR:** Use VR journaling tools to reflect on the sensory empathy experiences.

Day 2: Sensory Empathy in Education

Objective: Students will explore the role of sensory empathy in educational settings and how it supports diverse learners.

Activities:

- **Educational Empathy Exploration:**
  - **Traditional:** Discuss the importance of sensory empathy in education and how it supports diverse learners.
  - **VR:** Use VR tools to simulate classroom scenarios that highlight sensory empathy, such as accommodating sensory sensitivities.

- **Teaching Strategies:**

  - **Traditional:** Develop teaching strategies that incorporate sensory empathy to support diverse learners.
  - **VR:** Use VR platforms to design and implement virtual lessons that accommodate sensory needs.

- **Case Study:**

  - **Traditional:** Study the case of Helen Keller, focusing on her educational journey and the role of sensory empathy.
  - **VR:** Use VR to explore virtual environments related to Helen Keller's life and discuss her impact.

- **Reflection:**

  - **Traditional:** Reflect on the educational empathy activities and their impact on understanding diverse learners.
  - **VR:** Use VR journaling tools to reflect on the educational empathy experiences.

Day 3: Sensory Empathy in Healthcare

Objective: Students will learn about the role of sensory empathy in healthcare and how it improves patient care.

Activities:

- **Healthcare Empathy Exploration:**
  - **Traditional:** Discuss the importance of sensory empathy in healthcare and how it improves patient care.
  - **VR:** Use VR tools to simulate healthcare scenarios that highlight sensory empathy, such as understanding patient discomfort.

- **Patient Care Role-Playing:**

  - **Traditional:** Engage in role-playing exercises to practice sensory empathy in patient care.
  - **VR:** Use VR platforms to simulate patient care scenarios and practice empathetic responses.

- **Case Study:**

  - **Traditional:** Study the case of Florence Nightingale, focusing on her empathetic approach to nursing and patient care.
  - **VR:** Use VR to explore virtual environments related to Florence Nightingale's work and discuss her impact.

- **Reflection:**

  - **Traditional:** Reflect on the healthcare empathy activities and their impact on understanding patient care.
  - **VR:** Use VR journaling tools to reflect on the healthcare empathy experiences.

Day 4: Sensory Empathy in the Arts

Objective: Students will explore how sensory empathy can be expressed through various forms of art and its impact on audiences.

Activities:

- **Artistic Empathy Exploration:**

    ○ **Traditional:** Discuss how sensory empathy can be expressed through different forms of art and its impact on audiences.

    ○ **VR:** Use VR tools to explore artistic expressions of sensory empathy in virtual galleries and exhibitions.

● Art Projects:

○ **Traditional:** Engage in art projects that focus on expressing sensory empathy, such as painting, sculpture, or digital art.

    ○ **VR:** Use VR platforms to create and share virtual art projects that promote sensory empathy.

● Case Study:

○ **Traditional:** Study the case of Vincent van Gogh, focusing on how his art expressed sensory experiences and empathy.

    ○ **VR:** Use VR to explore virtual galleries of van Gogh's work and discuss his artistic expression.

● Reflection:

○ **Traditional:** Reflect on the artistic empathy activities and their impact on understanding and expressing sensory empathy.

    ○ **VR:** Use VR journaling tools to reflect on the artistic experiences.

Week 38 Lesson Plans

Day 1: Sensory Empathy in Communication

Objective: Students will learn about the role of sensory empathy in communication and how it enhances understanding.

Activities:

- **Sensory Empathy Exploration:**

  ○ **Traditional:** Discuss the concept of sensory empathy and how it enhances communication.

  ○ **VR:** Use VR tools to simulate communication scenarios where sensory empathy is crucial, such as understanding non-verbal cues.

- **Role-Playing Exercises:**

  ○ **Traditional:** Engage in role-playing exercises to practice sensory empathy in various communication settings.

  ○ **VR:** Use VR platforms to simulate sensory experiences and practice empathetic communication.

- **Case Study:**

  ○ **Traditional:** Study the case of Helen Keller, focusing on her communication methods and the role of sensory empathy.

  ○ **VR:** Use VR to explore virtual environments related to Helen Keller's life and discuss her impact.

- **Reflection:**

  ○ **Traditional:** Reflect on the sensory empathy activities and their impact on understanding communication.

  ○ **VR:** Use VR journaling tools to reflect on the sensory empathy experiences.

Day 2: Sensory Empathy in Teamwork

Objective: Students will explore the role of sensory empathy in teamwork and how it enhances collaboration.

Activities:

- **Teamwork Empathy Exploration:**
  - **Traditional:** Discuss the importance of sensory empathy in teamwork and how it enhances collaboration.
  - **VR:** Use VR tools to simulate teamwork scenarios that highlight sensory empathy, such as accommodating sensory sensitivities.

- **Team-Building Exercises:**
  - **Traditional:** Engage in team-building activities that promote sensory empathy and collaboration.
  - **VR:** Use VR platforms to simulate team-building exercises and practice empathetic teamwork.

- **Case Study:**
  - **Traditional:** Study the case of the Apollo 13 mission, focusing on how sensory empathy played a role in the teamwork and problem-solving.
  - **VR:** Use VR to explore virtual environments related to the Apollo 13 mission and discuss its impact.

- **Reflection:**
  - **Traditional:** Reflect on the teamwork empathy activities and their impact on understanding collaboration.
  - **VR:** Use VR journaling tools to reflect on the teamwork empathy experiences.

Day 3: Sensory Empathy in Community Engagement

Objective: Students will learn about the role of sensory empathy in community engagement and how it fosters inclusivity.

Activities:

- **Community Engagement Empathy Exploration:**
    - ○ **Traditional:** Discuss the importance of sensory empathy in community engagement and how it fosters inclusivity.
    - ○ **VR:** Use VR tools to simulate community engagement scenarios that highlight sensory empathy, such as public events.

- **Engagement Projects:**

○ **Traditional:** Plan and engage in community projects that promote sensory empathy and inclusivity.

- ○ **VR:** Use VR platforms to design and implement virtual community engagement projects.

- **Case Study:**

○ **Traditional:** Study the case of the Special Olympics, focusing on how sensory empathy is integrated into their events.

- ○ **VR:** Use VR to explore virtual environments related to the Special Olympics and discuss their impact.

- **Reflection:**

○ **Traditional:** Reflect on the community engagement empathy activities and their impact on understanding inclusivity.

- ○ **VR:** Use VR journaling tools to reflect on the community engagement experiences.

Day 4: Sensory Empathy in Environmental Awareness

Objective: Students will explore how sensory empathy can enhance environmental awareness and stewardship.

Activities:

- **Environmental Empathy Exploration:**
  - **Traditional:** Discuss how sensory empathy can enhance environmental awareness and stewardship.
  - **VR:** Use VR tools to explore environmental issues and observe sensory experiences in nature.

- **Stewardship Projects:**

  - **Traditional:** Engage in projects that promote environmental stewardship and sensory empathy, such as nature walks.
  - **VR:** Use VR platforms to simulate environmental projects and visualize their impact.

- **Case Study:**

  - **Traditional:** Study the case of Jane Goodall, focusing on her empathetic approach to environmental conservation.
  - **VR:** Use VR to explore virtual environments related to Jane Goodall's work and discuss her impact.

- **Reflection:**

  - **Traditional:** Reflect on the environmental empathy activities and their impact on understanding stewardship.
  - **VR:** Use VR journaling tools to reflect on the environmental empathy experiences.

Week 39 Lesson Plans

Day 1: Sensory Empathy in Conflict Resolution

Objective: Students will learn about the role of sensory empathy in conflict resolution and how it enhances understanding and cooperation.

Activities:

- **Conflict Resolution Empathy Exploration:**
  - **Traditional:** Discuss the importance of sensory empathy in conflict resolution and how it enhances understanding and cooperation.
  - **VR:** Use VR tools to simulate conflict scenarios that highlight sensory empathy, such as understanding sensory triggers.

- **Mediation Role-Playing:**

  - **Traditional:** Engage in role-playing exercises to practice sensory empathy in conflict resolution.
  - **VR:** Use VR platforms to simulate mediation sessions and practice empathetic responses.

- **Case Study:**

  - **Traditional:** Study the case of Mahatma Gandhi, focusing on his empathetic approach to conflict resolution and non-violence.
  - **VR:** Use VR to explore virtual environments related to Mahatma Gandhi's work and discuss his impact.

- **Reflection:**

  - **Traditional:** Reflect on the conflict resolution empathy activities and their impact on understanding and resolving disputes.

○ **VR:** Use VR journaling tools to reflect on the conflict resolution experiences.

Day 2: Sensory Empathy in Social Justice

Objective: Students will explore the role of sensory empathy in social justice movements and advocacy.

Activities:

- **Social Justice Empathy Exploration:**
  ○ **Traditional:** Discuss the importance of sensory empathy in social justice and how it drives advocacy.
  ○ **VR:** Use VR tools to explore social justice movements and observe sensory empathy in advocacy.

- ## Advocacy Projects:

  ○ **Traditional:** Plan and engage in projects that promote social justice and sensory empathy.
  ○ **VR:** Use VR platforms to design and implement advocacy projects in virtual environments.

- ## Case Study:

  ○ **Traditional:** Study the case of Martin Luther King Jr., focusing on his empathetic approach to civil rights advocacy.
  ○ **VR:** Use VR to explore virtual environments related to Martin Luther King Jr.'s work and discuss his impact.

- ## Reflection:

  ○ **Traditional:** Reflect on the social justice empathy activities and their impact on understanding and promoting empathy.
  ○ **VR:** Use VR journaling tools to reflect on the social justice experiences.

Day 3: Sensory Empathy in Creative Writing

Objective: Students will explore how sensory empathy can be expressed through creative writing and storytelling.

Activities:

- **Creative Writing Techniques:**
  - **Traditional:** Discuss techniques for expressing sensory empathy through creative writing and storytelling.
  - **VR:** Use VR tools to create immersive storytelling experiences that highlight sensory empathy.

- **Writing Projects:**
  - **Traditional:** Engage in creative writing projects that focus on expressing sensory empathy, such as short stories or poems.
  - **VR:** Use VR platforms to create and share virtual stories that promote sensory empathy.

- **Case Study:**
  - **Traditional:** Study the case of Maya Angelou, focusing on how her writing expresses sensory experiences and empathy.
  - **VR:** Use VR to explore virtual environments related to Maya Angelou's work and discuss her impact.

- **Reflection:**
  - **Traditional:** Reflect on the creative writing activities and their impact on understanding and expressing sensory empathy.
  - **VR:** Use VR journaling tools to reflect on the creative writing experiences.

Day 4: Sensory Empathy in Global Citizenship

Objective: Students will learn about the role of sensory empathy in global citizenship and how it helps address global challenges.

Activities:

- **Global Citizenship Empathy Exploration:**
  - **Traditional:** Discuss what it means to be a global citizen and the importance of sensory empathy in global contexts.
  - **VR:** Use VR platforms to explore global issues and the role of sensory empathy in addressing them.

- ## Global Challenges Activities:

  - **Traditional:** Engage in activities that address global challenges, such as climate change or poverty.
  - **VR:** Use VR tools to simulate global scenarios and practice sensory empathetic problem-solving.

- ## Case Study:

  - **Traditional:** Study the case of Malala Yousafzai, focusing on her role as a global citizen and advocate for education.
  - **VR:** Use VR to explore virtual environments related to Malala Yousafzai's work and discuss her impact.

- ## Reflection:

  - **Traditional:** Reflect on the global citizenship empathy activities and their impact on understanding global empathy.
  - **VR:** Use VR journaling tools to reflect on the global citizenship experiences.

Week 40 Lesson Plans

Day 1: Celebrating Empathy and Inclusion

Objective: Students will celebrate their journey of learning empathy and inclusion, reflecting on their growth and achievements.

Activities:

- **Empathy and Inclusion Showcase:**
    - **Traditional:** Create a showcase where students present their favorite projects and experiences from the curriculum.
    - **VR:** Use VR platforms to create a virtual gallery where students can display their projects and share their experiences.

- **Reflection Circle:**

    - **Traditional:** Hold a reflection circle where students share their most impactful moments and lessons learned.
    - **VR:** Use VR tools to create a virtual reflection space where students can share their stories and reflections.

- **Guest Speaker:**

    - **Traditional:** Invite a guest speaker who has made significant contributions to empathy and inclusion.
    - **VR:** Use VR to bring in a virtual guest speaker or explore a virtual talk by an inspiring figure in empathy and inclusion.

- **Reflection:**

    - **Traditional:** Reflect on the showcase and guest speaker, discussing the impact of empathy and inclusion on their lives.
    - **VR:** Use VR journaling tools to reflect on the celebration and share their thoughts.

Day 2: Empathy in Action

Objective: Students will put their empathy skills into action through community service and advocacy projects.

Activities:

- **Community Service Projects:**
  - **Traditional:** Plan and engage in community service projects that promote empathy and inclusion.
  - **VR:** Use VR platforms to design and implement virtual community service projects.

- **Advocacy Campaigns:**
  - **Traditional:** Develop advocacy campaigns that address social issues and promote empathy.
  - **VR:** Use VR tools to create virtual advocacy campaigns and share them with a wider audience.

- **Case Study:**
  - **Traditional:** Study the case of Malala Yousafzai, focusing on her advocacy for education and empathy.
  - **VR:** Use VR to explore virtual environments related to Malala Yousafzai's work and discuss her impact.

- **Reflection:**
  - **Traditional:** Reflect on the community service and advocacy activities, discussing their impact on empathy and inclusion.
  - **VR:** Use VR journaling tools to reflect on the empathy in action experiences.

Day 3: Empathy Through Storytelling

Objective: Students will explore the power of storytelling to convey empathy and inspire change.

Activities:

- **Storytelling Workshops:**
  - **Traditional:** Conduct workshops where students learn techniques for empathetic storytelling.
  - **VR:** Use VR tools to create immersive storytelling experiences that highlight empathetic themes.

- **Storytelling Projects:**
  - **Traditional:** Engage in storytelling projects that focus on expressing empathy, such as writing, theater, or digital media.
  - **VR:** Use VR platforms to create and share virtual stories that promote empathy.

- **Case Study:**
  - **Traditional:** Study the case of Chimamanda Ngozi Adichie, focusing on how her storytelling promotes empathy and understanding.
  - **VR:** Use VR to explore virtual environments related to Chimamanda Ngozi Adichie's work and discuss her impact.

- **Reflection:**
  - **Traditional:** Reflect on the storytelling activities and their impact on understanding and expressing empathy.
  - **VR:** Use VR journaling tools to reflect on the storytelling experiences.

Day 4: Vision for the Future

Objective: Students will envision how they can continue to practice and promote empathy and inclusion in their future endeavors.

Activities:

● **Vision Board Creation:**

○ **Traditional:** Create vision boards that represent their goals for practicing and promoting empathy and inclusion.

○ **VR:** Use VR tools to design virtual vision boards and share their future aspirations.

● **Future Planning Workshops:**

○ **Traditional:** Conduct workshops where students plan how they will continue to apply empathy and inclusion in their lives.

○ **VR:** Use VR platforms to simulate future scenarios and practice empathetic decision-making.

● **Case Study:**

○ **Traditional:** Study the case of Nelson Mandela, focusing on his vision for a more empathetic and inclusive world.

○ **VR:** Use VR to explore virtual environments related to Nelson Mandela's work and discuss his impact.

● **Reflection:**

○ **Traditional:** Reflect on their vision boards and future plans, discussing how they will continue to foster empathy and inclusion.

○ **VR:** Use VR journaling tools to reflect on their future aspirations and commitments.

Day 5: Grand Finale Celebration

Objective: Students will celebrate their journey and achievements in empathy and inclusion with a grand finale event.

Activities:

- **Celebration Event:**

    ○ **Traditional:** Organize a celebration event with performances, presentations, and awards to honor students' achievements.

    ○ **VR:** Use VR platforms to host a virtual celebration event where students can showcase their work and celebrate together.

- ## Awards Ceremony:

○ **Traditional:** Hold an awards ceremony to recognize students' contributions and growth in empathy and inclusion.

    ○ **VR:** Use VR tools to create a virtual awards ceremony and present awards to students.

- ## Guest Performances:

○ **Traditional:** Invite guest performers who inspire empathy and inclusion through their art.

    ○ **VR:** Use VR to bring in virtual performances or explore inspiring performances in virtual environments.

- ## Reflection:

○ **Traditional:** Reflect on the celebration event, discussing their journey and achievements in empathy and inclusion.

    ○ **VR:** Use VR journaling tools to reflect on the grand finale and share their thoughts.

Closing Remarks for Miss Jess's VR Empathy and Inclusion Curriculum

Dear Students,

As we reach the end of this incredible journey together, I want to take a moment to reflect on the path we've walked and the growth we've experienced. This curriculum was born from a deep passion for empathy, inclusion, and the transformative power of education. It has been a labor of love, inspired by my own story and the belief that each of you has the potential to make a profound impact on the world.

Throughout these weeks, we've explored the many facets of empathy, from understanding diverse perspectives to practicing compassionate communication. We've delved into the realms of politics, business, science, literature, and beyond, always with the goal of fostering a more inclusive and empathetic world. Your dedication, creativity, and openness have been truly inspiring.

Empathy is not just a skill; it's a way of being. It's about seeing the world through the eyes of others, feeling their joys and sorrows, and acting with kindness and understanding. It's about breaking down barriers and building bridges, creating a world where everyone feels valued and heard.

As you move forward, I encourage you to carry the lessons of empathy and inclusion with you. Use them in your daily interactions, in your communities, and in your future endeavors. Remember that every small act of kindness can ripple out and create positive change. You have the power to make a difference, to be a beacon of empathy in a world that often needs it.

Thank you for embarking on this journey with me. Your enthusiasm and commitment have made this curriculum come alive in ways I could only dream of. I am incredibly proud of each and every one of you. Keep shining your light, keep spreading empathy, and keep making the world a better place.

With heartfelt gratitude and best wishes for your future, Miss Jess

Sources Cited

1. **Proud to be Primary**. (n.d.). *Teaching Empathy: The Best Way to a Compassionate Classroom*. Retrieved from Proud[1]to[2]be[3]Primary[4].

2. **PBS NewsHour Classroom**. (2017, June 8). *Lesson Plan: Build Empathy with Stories about Disabilities*. Retrieved from PBS NewsHour[5].

3. **Whole Child Counseling**. (n.d.). *Free Social Emotional Learning Curriculum, Programs, Training, and Lesson Plans*. Retrieved from Whole Child[6] Counseling[7].

4. **Palacio, R.J.** (2012). *Wonder*. Alfred A. Knopf.

5. **Woodson, J.** (2012). *Each Kindness*. Nancy Paulsen Books.

6. **Mindful Schools**. (n.d.). *Mindfulness Curriculum for Schools*. Retrieved from Mindful Schools.

7. **Common Sense Media**. (n.d.). *Digital Citizenship Curriculum*. Retrieved from Common Sense Media.

---

1. https://proudtobeprimary.com/teaching-empathy/

2. https://proudtobeprimary.com/teaching-empathy/

3. https://proudtobeprimary.com/teaching-empathy/

4. https://proudtobeprimary.com/teaching-empathy/

5. https://www.pbs.org/newshour/classroom/lesson-plans/2017/06/lesson-plan-build-empathy-with-disabilities-stories

6. https://www.wholechildcounseling.com/post/free-social-emotional-learning-curriculum-programs-training-and-lesson-plans

7. https://www.wholechildcounseling.com/post/free-social-emotional-learning-curriculum-programs-training-and-lesson-plans

8. Collaborative for Academic, Social, and Emotional Learning (CASEL). (n.d.).

SEL Framework. Retrieved from CASEL.

9. **Empatico**. (n.d.). *Empathy-Building Activities for Classrooms*. Retrieved from Empatico.

10. **UNICEF**. (n.d.). *Teaching Respect and Empathy*. Retrieved from UNICEF.

11. **Making Caring Common**. (n.d.). *How to Build Empathy and Strengthen Your School Community*. Retrieved from Making[8]Caring[9]Common[10].

12. **TechNotes Blog**. (n.d.). *Six Strategies for Building Empathy in the Classroom*. Retrieved from TechNotes Blog[11].

13. **Humane Education**. (2018, August 27). *9 Strategies for Cultivating Empathy and Compassion in Your Classroom*. Retrieved from Humane Education[12].

14. **Twinkl**. (n.d.). *How to Teach Empathy in the Classroom: 7 Top Tips*. Retrieved from Twinkl[13].

15. **CommonLit**. (2022, August 9). *Stories & Texts About Disabilities to Teach Empathy & Inclusion*. Retrieved from CommonLit[14].

---

8.   https://mcc.gse.harvard.edu/resources-for-educators/how-build-empathy-strengthen-school-community

9.   https://mcc.gse.harvard.edu/resources-for-educators/how-build-empathy-strengthen-school-community

10.   https://mcc.gse.harvard.edu/resources-for-educators/how-build-empathy-strengthen-school-community

11.   https://blog.tcea.org/what-empathy-how-practice-empathy-classroom/

12.   https://humaneeducation.org/9-strategies-for-cultivating-empathy-and-compassion-in-your-classroom/

13.   https://bing.com/search?q=Teaching%2BEmpathy%3a%2BThe%2BBest%2BWay%2Bto%2Ba%2BCompassionate%2BClassroom

16. **Jennifer Findley**. (n.d.). *Teaching Empathy and Perspective in Grades 4-5 (Free Activities)*. Retrieved from Jennifer Findley[15].

17. **CEE-MAEC**. (n.d.). *Build Empathy with Stories About Disabilities – Lesson Plans*. Retrieved from CEE-MAEC[16].

18. **Second Step**. (n.d.). *SEL Activities and Resources*. Retrieved from Second[17] Step[18].

19. **University of New Hampshire Extension**. (n.d.). *Social, Emotional and Mindful Learning Curriculum: No Cost, Free!*. Retrieved from University[19]of[20] New Hampshire Extension[21].

---

14.   https://www.commonlit.org/blog/8-texts-featuring-characters-with-disabilities/

15.   https://jenniferfindley.com/teaching-empathy/

16.   https://cee-maec.org/resource/build-empathy-with-stories-about-disabilities-lesson-plans/

17.   https://www.secondstep.org/free-sel-resources

18.   https://www.secondstep.org/free-sel-resources

19.   https://extension.unh.edu/resource/social-emotional-and-mindful-learning-curriculum-no-cost-free

20.   https://extension.unh.edu/resource/social-emotional-and-mindful-learning-curriculum-no-cost-free

21.   https://extension.unh.edu/resource/social-emotional-and-mindful-learning-curriculum-no-cost-free

Don't miss out!

Visit the website below and you can sign up to receive emails whenever Miss Jess publishes a new book. There's no charge and no obligation.

https://books2read.com/r/B-A-VEWJC-NKCWE

BOOKS 2 READ

Connecting independent readers to independent writers.

About the Author

Jess Toft is a dedicated mother of two daughters, one of whom is on the autism spectrum. With a passion for creating educational curriculums that foster empathy and inclusion, she has developed the innovative "Miss Jess VR" curriculum. This program is designed to promote understanding and acceptance through immersive virtual reality experiences.

Drawing from her personal experiences and professional expertise, Jess is committed to making a positive impact in the world. She believes in the power of technology and innovation to bring about meaningful change, particularly in the fields of education and social inclusion.

In addition to her work on "Miss Jess VR," Jess is an advocate for sustainable fashion and global unity. She strives to create a better future for her children and for all children by promoting values of empathy, respect, and environmental stewardship.

When she's not working on her curriculum, Jess enjoys spending time with her family, exploring new technologies, and engaging with communities to spread her message of kindness and inclusion.

Read more at https://thinkngrowbig.com/.